by Eileen Myles

The Irony of the Leash (1978)
A Fresh Young Voice from the Plains (1981)
Sappho's Boat (1982)
Bread & Water (1987)
1969 (1989)
Not Me (1991)
Chelsea Girls (1994)
Maxfield Parrish / Early & New Poems (1995)

EILEEN MYLES

MAXFIELD PARRISH
EARLY & NEW POEMS

BLACK SPARROW PRESS · SANTA ROSA · 1995

ACKNOWLEDGMENTS

Some of these poems originally appeared in *Out There, Hero, 432 Review, Roof, dodgems, Partisan Review, Telephone, The Poetry Project Newsletter, Ladies Museum, Poets, Broadway, Synchro Harbor, Little Caesar, Little Light, Coming Attractions: American Poets in their Twenties, Gay and Lesbian Poets in Our Time, Uplate/American Poetry since 1970, Shiny, The New Censorship, Hanging Loose, New Directions, City, Kenyon Review, Art & Understanding, Outweek, Santa Monica Review, Lingo, O Anthology, Bombay Gin, Irregular, Radical Chick, The World, Pinched Nerve, Documents, Empathy, That Various Field/for James Schuyler, Aloud/voices from the Nuyorican poets cafe, Croton Bug, Scarlet, Caprice* and *Disclosure*.

The following poems have been recorded on CDs, LPs and cassettes: "Memorial," "I always put my pussy," "Warrior," "Rape" and "Debate With a Glove" are on *Move Into Villa Villakula*, villa villakula records, 230a Tremont St. #3, Boston, Mass. 02116, 1995. "Life" is on *The Nuyorican Symphony Live at the Knitting Factory*. "Tuesday Brightness" on *Big Ego*, Giorno Poetry Systems, 1978. "Lorna & Vicki" on *Sugar, Alcohol, & Meat*, The Dial-A-Poem Poets, Giorno Poetry Systems, 1980.

The Irony of the Leash was published by Jim Brodey Books, NYC, 1978. Thanks Jim.
A Fresh Young Voice from the Plains was published by Power Mad Books, NYC, 1981. Thanks to Barbara Barg who plays in Homer Erotic.
Sappho's Boat was published by Little Caesar Press, Los Angeles, 1982. Dennis Cooper, natch. To all these visionary poet/publishers I express my eternal gratitude.

Cover art by Nicole Eisenman.

Black Sparrow Press books are printed on acid-free paper.

LIBRARY OF CONGRESS CATALOGING-IN-PUBLICATION DATA

Myles, Eileen, 1949-
    Maxfield Parrish: early & new poems / Eileen Myles.
      p.   cm.
    ISBN 0-87685-975-9 (cloth trade: alk. paper). — ISBN 0-87685-974-0 (pbk. : alk. paper). — ISBN 0-87685-976-7 (signed cloth : alk. paper)
    I. Title.
PS3563.Y498M38   1995   95-8852
                                                CIP

For Jennifer

TABLE OF CONTENTS

MAXFIELD PARRISH (1995)

MAXFIELD PARRISH

Often I turn on people
in rather strange &
inexplicable ways.
The source of
the irritation
escapes me.
It always has.
Sometimes
my heart just
opens and
all the lions
get called
back to some
other corner
of the cave.
You'd probably
laugh at the
flowers I
bought tonight.
Bluish purple
& they don't
even have
a name. "Name?"
pronounced the
man at the
fruit stand
he shook
his head
& laughed.

These purple
flowers have
no name. &
no smell. But

the room
smelled & looked
different when
I brought them
in with me.
For instance
I was gentle
with their
stems while
I thought
about how
many lovers
have told
me I'm
rough. These
are hearty
thick stems
yet I slipped
the elastic
off their
limbs as
if I were
a servant
undressing
the president's
child. Just
thinking of her
for once. Oddly
alive & being
touched by
me in this
practical way.
The whole thing's
off-kilter the
way my purple
flowers grow.
Something that
makes sense
in February.
I have enough sense

14

to buy flowers
now. But such
strange ones.
Sprayed. Their
eerie color
is not real.
At least not all of it.
Maybe none of
it. The eerie
little branches
from which
piney green leaves
grow & I guess
that's real. But
the 287,
no I mean
thousands
of faintly blue bells
I can hardly see
I must be getting old
up close they make me feel dizzy
the fineness, the wealth of this pseudo-life
tiny balls, pale blue
with a sliver of a tongue
sticking out or sometimes
everything's teeny & sexual
it's sort of like underpants
a cover or a case
that's purple & the little
ball is blue.
I don't know why this wave
of a plant belongs in my vase.
I needed something fake to
start me up. Something
I could be gentle
with just to try.
Looking hard I say Baby
I don't know why I can
give you everything
& I'm dazzled by your frown.

The Windsor Trail

Pines at attention
spotted rocks

some things
are more
beautiful
when you
approach
them through
shade

you think it's
water bubbling
over the rocks but
it's light.

Lady Eileen
wants to
rest in your
decision
like the
rocks piled
up on
the side
of the
road

or the
sound of
distant
water.

Lady Eileen
wants to

rest in your
decision
little plants

but why is a
tree occasionally
skinned

the rolling cluck
of a bird
in there

Lady Eileen
wants to rest
in your
decision
trees & money

the welcoming
path

and the
mountain
hovers

Lady Eileen
wants to
rest in
your shade

the flies
all pulling
their tender
strings

and the roots
go who
knows
where.

I bet a
rock thinks.
What else
would it
be doing
for all
this time

white jutting
out in
the middle of
trees

full of
thought
in the
sun

part of the
pine tree
is blue

golden flowers

Lady Eileen
wants to
make the
acquaintance
of your
rocks & birds

the wounded-
eye dead
trees

a live pine
surrounded by
aspen

zillions of eyes
in the light

lead me down
now butterfly
I need
some
water

I need
the falling
depths
of these
views

the bluefingered
trees

black pinecombs
in the
shade

and a huge
pile of
shit from
what animal

mustard moss

and the meat
of the
fallen tree,
turkey

I intend
to walk
this way
forever

Lady Eileen
wants to
rest in
your decision
a huge
dark nest
hanging
low in
your branches

I get it!
the bottom
of a tree
is a fountain
a god
spinning
out

the mellow sound
of bending
aspens

crash, a
giant, dead
at your
foot, and
years of
moss growing
over

this whole area
is a catastrophe
of fallen
trees

years
ago some
storm
that the
wind remembers

20

some trees
are a violent
grey, thin
twisted
spitting green
leaves at
its top

or
young & thin
with heart
shaped leaves

I don't know
if we can
find our
way back
to some
deep erotic
place

can't we be like
the beautiful
aspen, a
million strong
the color
of growth
itself
sort of tan
sort of
green
deeply white

wait for that
man to
turn the
corner so
I can
kiss
this tree

Believe me
when the
sun's bright
or in the
shadows
I am
an instrument
a plant
as true
as a
rock

will everyone
stand
and grow
over me
when I
die.

Let me
rest in
your decision
but I
want to
die in
a storm,
struck
down &
covered
with
moss—
without a
name, more
dignified
than that,
Tree!

Lady Eileen
would like
to pee

on your
decision.
How far
can I stray
from the
path?

Crouching
as I wet
the grass
& the rocks

a woman
going down

moss growing
between her
legs

these are
aspen and the wounds
and the
eyes

I walk

the urgency
of that bird
something being
turned

what astounds
me in the
forest is
the living
and dead
are side
by side

a fallen

tree spends
years
leaning

the dead
lean gently
on life

and dead,
with their
peculiar
changes,
they almost
have names

thin split
fallen,
open head,
long dive,
rumpled

while the
live are
standing.
Their silent
listening
to a
sound

now the
rocks
have solved
all this

always being
different
or less

they make
me think
of violins

these aspen—

I'm walking
through
a string
section

later a
rape, a burnt
catastrophe.
Dead from
the crotch
the damaged
legs spindling
up

Lady Eileen
wants to
rest in
your decisions

it lightens
and I
hear a
brook

you have
to learn
to play
yourself

even in
silence

here's a
fence to
prevent
a fall

into the

rocky
stream

pink rocks
and roots
black mud

if it
doesn't
come in
words

the big blue
mountain

leave room

it doesn't
mean it
didn't
happen.

NEW POEM

My lover came over my house
one afternoon—I was doing
a big mailing for a show—
the one before this. She
was crying and I was trying
to make her happy. I was
sitting on the floor in this
sand chair we bought to go
camping last summer. I
was sitting there counting all
the people in the zip code
one thousand three. Myra
announced she was leaving
and I started to do a
little dance from my
chair—I was making
faces and had paws
it was a little dog dance
I explained to her. It's
a little dog chorus line.
A show about a chorus
line of dogs. But dog
chorus lines are irregular.
They just wander all over
the city, stray dogs.
Related but not you
know doing anything in
sync, but shitting eating
pissing fucking   just having
a dog life. That kind
of chorus. It's a
very modern art, the
dog chorus line and
I thought about all

the dogs on my lap I was
mailing my postcards to.
Eventually we got sick of
the shape of that kind
of dog chorus line. It
was true, but there's
so much of that, truth,
and it's so irregular so
we decided to make something
new—dogs in saddles,
dogs sprayed blue &
gilded, you know arranged
in galleries or groupings.
The irony of that kind
of product, an external
order, that's the joke,
despite the fact the
dogs are still roaming
around hungry &
hopeless, we're getting
very involved with
the new blue dogs
God, now we can decorate
them so many different
ways and we feel
so hopeless about
life, what can we
really do, so we
find another funny
way to arrange the
dogs, make a big
show, act as if
just for a second you
can have some kind of control,
and it is kind of funny, I
mean dogs aren't blue

BLEEDING HEARTS

Know what
I'm jealous of?
Last night.
It held
us both
in its
big black
arms
& today
I hold
between
my legs
a shivering
pussy.
Bleeding &
shaking
wet with
memory
grief &
relief.
I don't know
why the universe
chose me
to be female
so much beauty
& pain,
so much
going on
inside
all this
change
everywhere
coins falling
all over

the bed
& death
is a dream.
Deep in
the night
with thousands
of lovers
the sucking
snapping
reeling
flesh
deep in
the cavity
of endless
night across
mounds
of bodies
I peer over
is it
love or
war. The hollow
creeping
cheek
where
I was
born.

RUT

I feel like a baby reading
a paper, an enormous
stranger pounding
between my legs.
She flies, a wolf,
she is green
sizzling, remarkable
she talks my
sex talk
she blows bubbles

the very chair
I sit upon
vibrates

at all the
issues in the world
she yawns
she is my baby
reading a paper
she turns me
red & brown
every creature
has its
smell for her
an easy violence
immense, stormy
waves rushing
over the
deck of
my rolling
ship

its little importances

my life. To her
it is nothing,
my pounding
goddess
drum beat,
no name

a furious dance
until I slip
into the
oblivion
of my
weeks & days

she sucks
the breath
from my
bones
she is water
underground
gooey
light

a cross
a spinning
stick

a treasure
commotion
the message
delivered
slowly

an ache
a stab
the lips of
the volcano
soft and
huge, the
lava flows

& she rolls
on hungry
turning
her head
seeking more
than the
building, people
hands, world
can give,
she caves
in, a monstrous
new &
holy
song.

SLEEPLESS

I came in tonight and my building sighed.
It was a beautiful woman stretching in
the morning. All blue and blonde and
gauzy white. My dreams of you are always
softer than you are. My dreams
must need a goddess and it seems she has
your face. And so you may stay a while
in my heart. My image of your languorous
arms and fists slowly stretching through
the early day as if Monday were another
sleepless woman's body. Two of you
to make the universe complete.
The embrace of you makes my day
so sweet because I am the author
of this sport. The other woman is dark
and green and curly, full of rocks
and sauce and dark lights hanging

in the sky. She's the sound of a
yawning cave. She pulls me down
and makes me whisper evil and
violent wishes, makes me spank
her with a whip and fierce
rules and fond names to cage
her in. How could everything
shrink so—these women dancing
in my mind. What holds the world together
for anyone else—blind women, white
men, frightened Chinese boys. I guess I
have a hunger that's stronger than
toast, I wouldn't say most
because the shapeless woman hanging
over my shoulder says I mustn't.
She shows me with her eyes which are water.

She tells me with her breath, incredible,
a hurricane, a disaster.
Her teeth are sparkling
ruin, her tongue a poison
snake, her throat
an endless fall
onto a meadow of warm sushi.
And lakes of blood and
green birds swooping
and singing.

And dawn, a dawn
that's unrecognizable.
It's there I finally
stopped in your
midnight arms.

What could lead
me this way,
what furry
balconies await me. What amber
yawns what plentiful breasts
diving between the legs
of God to see a mirror
an amazing pond, a one-eyed
man inside you cleaning
the kitchen with a sparkling
knife. I step on his face
and snap his back in two
with my finger and
you reward me with
hearthrob and
I never do come back.
I want you home with
me. I want you alone
with me. I wish you
would get lost
so I could walk the world
with my women.
I would call your name

everywhere. Wouldn't
that be enough, even
better. There is a woman
in the flower. Millions
of women hiding in the trees.
You will never miss me.
There is a universe
of color for you to
feed from. Before
I leave you I will
open its legs
with my sword.

CRAZY

As a result of my time
spent in nature—the purpling
sky, the soap-colored sage
the silver scar of the river
across the land, a hairy-backed
island pushing out, into the water
and of course the bushy grey clouds
among which wiggles a tiny
white light, one star, or
worse a UFO to change
these depths to spectacle ...

As a result of my time spent
in nature, and everything
changes in a minute or so,
add a day & everything's different
a sky scraped clean of clouds
and nearly lilac over
hills that used to be red.
So my legs are crossed
on the perfect rock
having run home fast to
get this pen, looking out on
a different night,
duller, but I know that
river now. Having been
all wet & covered with mud
but I crossed it, and
thought that would solve
my problem. It has,
sort of. I became
a follower of children,
their walks that get
you lost & dizzy.

I read fat & stupid
novels, became the
hero, usually male, & changed
my life like that. But
now these birds are laughing
at me & I only pass through
states I once wrote for
catalogues from, hoping
Montana or Wisconsin
could make me me which
40 years of life haven't
done, but one of those
degrees could've, one of those
life-long student loans
instead of my endless
New York debt, for trips
and meals. I was only
trying to please you. Like
the star in the sky I'm
completely alone. And only
a fool is alone in nature,
the thing I think I
was trying to buy, me
then in a funny hat,
being different, faraway.

To the Maiden of Choice

Too many systems colliding
in the skies. A man
walks in and he chose
to die, chose to be
homosexual and a man,
chose the parents
who seeded him so,
chose to be born
now, in a plague.

This is where the New Age
grows fascist:
I see, therefore
I am. A harmonic
convergence of those
who choose, the unvisioning
leading greasy corporal lives
prey to disease, doubt
and age. In my
straw hat and my
Indian shawl I feed
sweets to the hummingbirds
from my blue house.
I drive a quaint
turquoise car and
heal myself, so
don't get in my way.

I have the capacity
to learn from
former lives. Perhaps
you don't—sitting
here hungry,
latching on to

a frail boat.

Perhaps the universe
is 68 years old.
At forty you're
neither famous
nor invisible,
poling for your
life, then idling
for months,
following a
color, a
woman, a
tree. If you
knew you
were a Trojan
woman, a sailor
from Crete, your
incompatible
sadness and
hunger might
at last become
friends. In tonight's
full moonery
in this vision of lolling
trees, you could
be one primate
seeing, then
being the
captain of
your hopeless
little boat.

Oh the night we
laughed at our luck.
We could've strangled
in the birth canal,
we could've OD'd,
drowned in Walden Pond,
been killed by a car on

Second Ave., cracked
my skull on the metal
stairs, been beaten
to mush by an
angry lover, smothered
by my brother, oh
the tremendous escape
that occurred and
delivered me to
this bright and
ambivalent
now.

I love paintings because
I didn't have to
paint them. The great
ones seem painted
by no one. Did
they choose to awaken
behind the brush,
in a flurry of
pigment and
vision.

I choose to eat
an old peach.
It's sitting here
in front of
my face. "Old"
tastes just
like alcohol.
You notice that?

The epidemic of
choice began
in my life
when I put
down my beer
and walked,
a free woman

not quite
32. I chose
to drink a
tremendous amount
of alcohol
in seventeen years
rather than sipping
away till 68
when I die.
Even today
my passionate sobriety
is fueled by my
freedom to drink.
I choose not
to. How do I
know I didn't
choose my parents.
Wouldn't my life,
my history be
strangely empowered
by the thought
of some non-carnate
me requesting dark-
haired Irish male,
alcoholic, Polish
female orphan,
sweet and
willful. Was I
turned on by them?
Was it some kind
of astral three-
some. Did I
think they would
bring me here
in exactly this
way: 8 o'clock
alone, New Mexican
Twilight, Pentel pen
on legal paper
and the crickets

creak and there's
trilling
too and the
boat of my
life is ready
to turn and
why did I
pick that
Irishman
now, or
Genevieve
except for their
love and their
interest in Opera
which I share
too. Both of
them had terrific
legs. Not the
money for front
row tickets,
nope standing room
but I've got these
legs! I stood on the
balcony of the
Santa Fe Opera
and watched the
eclipsing moon.
It was a painting
and I wanted
to paint. I
wanted to pick
up the brush
and embody that
stylish scene:
two blond boys
with bangs and
tans, tall &
thin, at the
ice of their
drinks as a

gleaming crescent
remained of
the moon. I
thought of
Neptune which
has a lunar
partner just
200,000 miles
away. How
huge it must
be in the
sky. Probably
no one to see
it there. And
where is Morris?
Did my parents
mean for me
to meet Morris?
Who knew Jane
Bowles and now
he knows me. He
name-drops in
an inclusive way.
When did you
come around? Did
you meet Frankie?
I would've picked
different parents
if I was meant
to meet Frankie.
I met Jimmy
and Ted. The
women won't
let me know
them, but
that's my choice.
I am beginning
to want to
know women.

Having ovaries
and uterus,
breasts, one
vagina and
a clit—
how could
I choose
to be alone
with men.

I met Susie
and Jane
and Robin
and Nancy
and Genevieve
and Zeborah
and Barbara
and Barbara
and Linda
and Reno and
Bonnie and
Patti and
Sarah. Now if
I'm getting it
right you don't
make one decision,
you make millions
of them. So say
you might have
picked fabulous
parents but then
you chose to
get polio so
you died. Or you
could have picked
the worst parents
on earth, say
Mr. & Mrs. William
F. Buckley and
nonetheless

picked no diseases
wonderful friends,
a good car and
you would be
deliriously happy
at this moment
driving through
town. Do I
think I picked
my parents. Yes.
Because as I stood
on my good-looking
legs watching
the moon
slide in and out of
the earth's shadow
I teetered on the
edge of awe and
artifice and
during the first
scene of Callisto
I was transformed.
My parents were
sad and funny
and strong.
But I did not
choose for Massachusetts
to have pines
and Plymouth Rock.
Neptune has
rings but not
by request. I think
I am not God
tonight. I am
different from
the rain. Do I
have power
over Nature?
Would I want
it? I don't

even like to
drive a shift.
It gives you
more control
but I want
less. My parents
were a poetic
decision. If I
was a librarian
I'd say it was
a matter of classification.
A matter of plumbing,
a nuclear decision.
Later on we get
a job, but each
of us is our
own little work.
And I don't believe
in God. On and
on it's a bigger
and bigger
womb. It's time
to know some
women and
come home.

*

I always put my pussy
in the middle of trees
like a waterfall
like a doorway to God
like a flock of birds.
I always put my lover's cunt
on the crest
of a wave
like a flag
that I can
pledge my
allegiance
to. This is my
country. Here,
when we're alone
in public.
My lover's pussy
is a badge
is a night stick
is a helmet
is a deer's face
is a handful
of flowers
is a waterfall
is a river
of blood
is a bible
is a hurricane
is a soothsayer.
My lover's pussy
is a battle cry
is a prayer
is lunch
is wealthy

is happy
is on teevee
has a sense of humor
has a career
has a cup of coffee
goes to work
meditates
is always alone
knows my face
knows my tongue
knows my hands
is an alarmist
has lousy manners
knows her mind

I always put
my pussy in the middle
of trees
like a waterfall
a piece of jewelry
that I wear
on my chest
like a badge
in America
so my lover & I
can be safe.

HOME

We don't live with rats but we look at them all the time. We live with them. Rats are black like the rails of the subway. You can hardly see them. It's almost one thing. In a man's life he was born and he lived and he was compassionate and then he died painfully and publicly and then he lived again. The message is that if we think of this man we won't mind dying. We will be just like him except when we live again we will live with him and his parents. It's interesting that the point of christianity is that when we die we won't really die. We will go live with him and he lived just so we could see what new kind of people we will soon be rooming with. It's like a play within a play isn't it, a major religion doing its demonstration within the context of history and human memory. It is all I want to think about. The world is always turning into a new kind of home based on the information I have received in the world. It seems to me I am always preparing for a beautiful death. Avoid all short-cuts. Dress the way you like. Always check the train schedule in advance. Pay your own way. Apologize for what you did, not what you didn't do. Don't be mad at the guitar player in the subway. Don't wait too long. Patience is relative. Read the paper. Keep throwing things out. Keep your life light and spacious. Expect to feel different. You might need a camera. There are puddles and angles you'll never want to forget. If you get scared, count. The dream you're seeing out the window might be death. I think God is death. I really do.

Shhh

I don't think
I can't afford the time to not sit right down &
write a poem about the heavy lidded
white rose I hold in my hand
I think of snow
a winter night in Boston, drunken waitress
stumble on a bus that careens through
Somerville the end of the line
where I was born, an old man
shaking me. He could've been my dad
You need a ride? Wait, he said.
This flower is so heavy in my hand.
He drove me home in his old blue
Dodge, a thermos next to me,
cigarette packs on the dash
so quiet like Boston is quiet
Boston in the snow. It's New York
plates are clattering on St. Mark's
Place. Should I call you?
Can I go home now
& work with this undelivered
message in my fingertips
It's summer.
I love you.
I'm surrounded by snow.

MEMORIAL

Bette Davis just died.
What has been Bette Davis is now nothing.

    She is dead.
While it must've been great to
be Bette Davis, now it
is no feeling.
The life of Bette Davis stopped,
so now she is something that
was great. Did you like Bette
Davis? How do you feel
about her now? She's just
history. Already. She's not going
to do something new. She
hadn't done something new
for a very long time.
When was she great. Let's
look at that part. Bette
Davis at her best without
her interfering, having her
own feelings about what
was good. Because what
people think about their
lives, about the part
that shows, and with
Bette Davis that was about
all there was—who
could trust or really
care about what a person
like that thinks. We can decide what
we really like and throw
the rest away. Just
like her body rotting in

the ground. Stinking and
no one around to smell
it. Probably buried in
very good clothes. Bare-
foot because nobody sees
that part. Picture yourself
in a coffin. Dead
and smelly. Give it a
little light so you
can really see. Think
of that weird face that
Bette Davis had,
those eyes rotting under
the ground. Think of her famous
face this week on the
cover of *People* magazine.
Her famous dead face.
Isn't it eerie. Even
when she was alive
it must've been a little
bit like being dead.
The picture, the face in
the frame of film was
the Bette Davis we know.
Now we can really truly
look at Bette Davis.
The star. Not the rot-
ting carcass in the ground.
Cause someday we'll be
there too. We need the glamourous
light of wonderful human
beings like Bette Davis
so we can forget that
nothing matters, really
& truly, nothing at
all. Except life. And
Bette Davis doesn't have
it anymore. We do.

REGINA COELI

Now when
I'm home
hunched
over the
phone
foot up
on some
indescribable
piece
of furniture
I'm back
in the
saddle
again
like
I sang
at the
bar when
I hoisted
a beer
to my
lips. But
I'm crazy
now
with
my sex
my age
the
autumnal
heat
my blues
which
have
blasted

to orange
this
moment
& for
this I
am ready
to thank
you Lady,
something
everyone.

THE MIRROR IS MY MOTHER

for Myra

If I'm not in there I'm in here
the city accordion in someone's kind
hands, squeeze in, pull out,
holds us closely on the couch.
The mirror is moved
and I'm facing the wall, let me turn
quickly and turn to the city. The beauty
of Christmas is accidental,

      a legion of scarves getting
off, and cars, paintings, movements,
a Cardinal aghast, turning the pages
of the *New York Times* they had lived
together for quite a few years
both happened to be standing there
when the Berlin wall fell down.

As I watched her lying there,
shrivelled, the huge head decorated
and the room swayed with candles
and white flowers and as I said
it was as if you moved a mirror
and what you saw was the wall
instead. My uncle's lips looked
rubber, smeared all over
his poor old Irish face.
It was his voice I knew, not his
lips. Poor old Uncle Tim who
wiggled his ears. Aunt Anne always
so huge in power and strength,
strangled by grief, a little
pooch, dependent on her grandchildren

56

who loved her. I say death is a strange
thing. I want to stay open to this
life, my rubber lips twisting
in lies and fear, my eyes burning
with impatience and truth.
An angel should come and they would
speak. On my birthday they were handing me
thousands of pictures of myself, as they
do in our culture, the clapping of
hands, lights, everything that's not
dead and dark. I brought my ancient
bunny home from Boston, the puppets
I brought my mask. Now this African woman
looks down on my life, poor and white
outside the christian lights blink
comically onto my tenement bed.
In East Friesia the lightning means
they're taking your picture again.
Don't squint, let your mother
look at your beautiful face and love
you for breath and movement and
hearing an animal suddenly moving
in the brush let it pass.
Never strike.

En Garde

All the hills & the trees
and the woman
chopping wood
outside &
the lazy
dog. I am
dedicated
to this. Its existence.
The marinade.
The veterans
of wars up the
hill popping
off their
guns, dreaming
of Iraq.
They can go
there
if they'd
like to
go. In a state of War
a man can
understand
what a woman
means by
space.
All the
homosexuals
are word-
processing.
Not going
to war.
All you
have
to say

is I'm Gay
& you can
stay in
America
forever. Just
think about
how it's
felt for
me to
be female
in America.
Or in
this world.
Any man
would
kill a
man,
certainly
be exonerated
in court
for killing
a man
who was
gay &
came on
to him
that way,
you know
sexual.

Every day
I get
treated
that way.
Mmm I like those tits.
Has George Bush
ever been
flattered
walking down
the streets

for his
big balls,
so scrumptious.

I look up
and I
face a square
of clouds
packed
in blue.
My friend
is so lucky
to own
this barn.
Am I in
America
while
I'm writing
this
poem?

My tongue &
lips are
in America.
So's my
brain my
female brain
so's my
dog who
I love.
My car,
that wreck,
my ultimate
female karma
spilling over
into the
male space
like acid
if they
had to

60

be me
for a
moment
the beauty &
the beast
they could
read my
face, they
would know
their place
they would
give me
space,
they would
lower their
guns &
beg for
water.

THREE WISHES

The tree shadow
is longer across
the lawn.
Longer than
when? the
last time
I sat
here. It
was earlier
in the summer
now it's
August
we go deeper
into the
year like
a knife
into an
apple
or a day
that
hurts so
much &
its beauty
is almost
gone.

PV

> *Today is so full, and yet*
> *today never gets spoiled.*
> —Tim Dlugos

Some old drunk who'd been
to France recently died, left
his collection of Isherwood, John
O'Hara, tobacco-stained, grungy
with tattered invites hanging out.
I come wagging out of the train
station at 59th & nearly scream,
Just the books I need!

I take my own sense of
abundance down
into the subway, the
F, Second Ave., the
bodies strewn, the
stink of human
shit the ungodly
lights, standing, waiting
in the heat.

The mother won't repeat
for the child. If you
didn't get it the first
time …

Who is that Irish novelist
he says, the one we see
in meetings in East Hampton

the train arrives & I hop

on, that lesbian poet, the
one we always see around
3:30 in Kiev, having a very
late lunch I guess.

We whiz uptown to get help.
We whiz back down. This
is an old fashioned phone
call, Do you have
10 bucks, All saints day 1989.

I slept with her last night,
first time since August, she's
moving so the smells of her
neighbor's pot won't waft
insidiously into her bedroom
anymore, Jan with his
new electric piano, Jan the
monkey-faced pot dealer who
teaches tai chi.

I went to see 17 art shows on
Saturday. 17. That's not a lot.
Saw Tim in the hospital on Sun-
day. Thin Tim. We know he'll
come out. He doesn't want to
be everyone's friend Tim who has AIDS
so we won't let him be that.
We won't.

We charged around in our
dungarees watching the century
approach. Another one, nicer
than this, young again, full
of conviction, naivete, covered
with hair and sunlight, brim-
ming with time, a wave of
invention ...

I take my sense of abundance

into the subway & what do
I see? People bending reading
swaying, torn posters
waving in a song of
sickening movement. Why don't
they think we know about
rice, racing ... handsome woman
fiddling with her bag. We're
the same people who met in
a disaster, but nothing hap-
pened here. You can't call
it joy this somnolence, licking
our lips with our earphones
on. The poet got off
in the yellowing light,
the rising tile, then
Lexington Ave. Have you
gone here, did you
go there everyone wants
to know. & there's the
EXIT. Absolutely now
I'm going & the buildings
are growing before my
eyes.

IMMANENCE

All the doors in my home are open.
There's a pulse outside I want to hear

The phone's unplugged.
The pastiche of you on me would be unforgivable now.

If there's a god squirming around
she sees me & is me.
I wish the birds were souls, invisible.
I wish they were what I think they are; pure sound.

LOOKING OUT, A SAILOR

The clouds looked made, & perhaps
they were. An angry little shelf
for the moon to have
some influence
on. I'm dying tomorrow

my car died tonight
a glorious explosion
then clunk.

Turning pages, turning pages
coming up on midnight
when the poet died.

It was his heart
not his
head.

The girl, she was say 27
covered in tattoo
a sauce her
boyfriend
made to cover
her sins

let's say she is glad tonight
to be dead. Her name?
Lorri Jackson.

So I push on & my
dog needs
a bath—don't sell Rosie
short says the
trainer & flattered

I won't.

I remember the last
night with my
car. Came home
& called the night
watery grave. Didn't
know why. Everyone
dying around
me now. But
not yet,
not me yet.

The lights all smeared &
gooey in an incredible
downpour like Lorri's
body I could see shadows
that I think were
persons, they were
the dead &
we were
alive, yes I think
it was that
way that
last night. So lucky
I didn't hit
one.

My pooch
by my side. This
is my life
when I grow
up I thought
as a child.
In my boat with
my dog, named
what, Rosie,
she barks
driving into
the night

68

god, we couldn't
see a thing
but we weren't
scared. Besides
we'd had
plenty of
life.

Prayed for a
parking space.
Funny turning
in the dark
those lights
back there
are cars I think.
Don't ask me
said Rosie.

But I wanted to sail
the rest of my
life. It was dumb.
I'd arrived
there was
my space.

Perfect & I pulled in
& this is the
saddest poem
I ever wrote.
What can I tell you about
sadness, the shapes
you find beneath it,
how you run from
it in your sleep,
bolting awake

early in my labors I
worked with
children, I was one
then but so

what the story goes.
Autistic kids, a
boy named
Bobby
who so loved
porcelain he leaned
his cheek on
it, a little
animal & his
cool white
mama

the things I warm my
hands by are not
true, someone
who holds her
head like
that forbidding
I think
is warm

I would lay my paw
on her icy bottle,
her icy dead
cheek, her red
legs

the red light rippled
in my watery grave
if I could paint
tonight I would
be the word
that fills the silence
after modern
following something
slow, red
changing lanes
it was utterly
silent my
painting, the

dog breathing
well, relentlessly
& they had
pulled my antennae
off long ago so
deep down
there was
some music
classical,
how to say
I was having
the pivotal
moment of
my life
with a
dog, all
the silence
had led up to
here & streamers
could be
followed to
the moment
of my
death,

what kind
could I be
some kind of
poet who
followed it
along, say it's
distant &
far off, or
right next
to me
now, I
do not know
or choose
to. I saw
the world

melt all
at once

I want to
go with
everyone
waiting for
everything
to shift back
to real &
it's stranger
& stranger
now—all
of my lies don't
lie anymore.
The car dies
& I drive
on. The rain
stops. He said
I would
surely outlive
my dog &
I know
that & I
took her
home. But
everyone. No I
didn't know
that. When
everyone
goes I
go. I'm
following
now, &
our truth
is dark

SURPRISE

Hey, you know
what I always
meant to
tell you. One
night I
got called
into work
late. Actually
I had
worked
earlier,
came home
walked
the dog
was eating
a cracker
with this
herb cheese
on it,
very salty
& they called
& said
do you
want to
work again
& I said
okay because
I'm broke
& the car took
me downtown
to Liberty
Plaza, the
21st floor
where I

goofed
off most of the
night reading
The New Yorker
—stuff I
never can
read at
home, slow,
& then
the document
came in
actually
it came
in trickles
so I was
up & down
all night
fighting
sleep, making
coffee, poking
around for
candy or
some kind
of food.
Balancing
my cup
I looked up
& the room
was sur-
rounded
by color
photographs,
vistas, bright
& hairy
plunging &
precise
by Eliot Porter
& I know
you love
him. I

74

kept meaning
to tell
you that.

KID'S SHOW: 1991

The tree
smells like
a lollipop
a dog barks
like a
bell. The
dog drinks
the tree's
water.

This is
nature
in the
city. Distorting
childhood
a woman
like a
well. The
phone ringing
endlessly
on the
horizon.

This
is time.
Technology
meets
a new
year.
Sun, moon
look
what
I made
up. Goodbye.

WEAVING

Her hand juts up, a claw
against the dirty
spotty geyser
of the window
pane, the
hasty juxta-
positions of
passing wires
& trees. It's angel
time. A row
of kids
in goofy
hats await
the passing train
& I am men
in hats. Missions
spraying around
the world. Packages
being brought to
Ankara. No, an
evasion of
some sort. To be
one of the
millions of
canals that
sear the
world. To
make
it Mars
to be the
string of
an angel
wrapping
the ball

of the earth
an armament
of the firmament
that's flying
through space
right now.
I am not
waiting. For
school, for
the book to
arrive. I'd like
to be, and
am, not
future past or
present. But
a deeper now
that speeds
it along. But
what to do with
your head
on my lap
while the
world speeds
by. What
to call
this stillness
in a mission
but love.

A DEBATE WITH A GLOVE

John Higgins, Mary McCluskey
what about them? I flashed
my palm and wagged it.
The personality as the
sight of spiritual advancement
what about my book?
Spirituality & Sexuality,
that's all. Make the young dogs
pay. A play is an opportunity
to do something visual.
My vision. Here let me straighten
these shirts. Eileen spoke
so well about the creative
process. Maybe she would
like to do it again.

What about those monuments?
The beggar & the priest.
The weight of my cunt.
Let me walk the streets of Baghdad.
Are these breasts mine?
What kind of problem is a poem.
We don't get to choose what
kind of spiritual experience we
have. We don't get to choose
our orgasm. We don't
even get to choose our
lover. What happened to me.
Who was she.
Are they bedbugs.
Take me to Delhi fast.
I itch.
At five my soul wants to be
alone. With the world &

its armies. With my
sex. With my hands
with my beautiful
hands. She had
been turned
into a deity
in the end.
First she vanished,
then she was
that.
I know what kind
of god
I'd like to be.
A blue god.
A blue god man.
Those men, they make
me want to dance.
Tell me something else.
Was I married.
Have I been here
before. Why am I
always in between.
Is it late or
is it early.
Money, I could
give a shit.
Fame, forget it.
An authenticity
that rattles
my bones. Is
it two of
everything
or one.
Is it none.
I'm sorry we
went to war
with you &
broke your
bridge.
I'll fix it now.

80

Really. Should
we get married
or something?
I'm very
smart. Oh
you don't
think so.
Well. Maybe
I'll write
a poem. Suddenly
I don't care
that I'm
gonna
die. Even
the bed keeps
me awake.
The breeze
of the world.
It opened
my jar.
It called
me home.
It said,
Lucifer!

THEKKADY

We're embarrassed to
look for animals in
the woods. I'd rather
sink or swim on my
own momentary personal
aesthetics than any
attempts at realism.
Those trees look good.
I'm too sophisticated.
That's my problem. I'm
stunned I bothered to
have a body at all
& that's why I
can't stop looking at
it. Like a cloud.

Our path is slow
& scarey. That's
why I wish
you were here
to see the elbows
in the trees. And
the slingshots.
What am I capable
of seeing on my
own besides
fire. A thousand
stairs lead me
to your temple.
The monkeys
in the trees
are watching.
Black 'n stretchy.
Like toys.

And I'm right,
that is fire.
This is not
the best
tour in town.

I'm looking for white trees.
Something new. I'm
looking for something
too stupendous
to report.
Something that stops
everything.
I used to think
it was the end
of the world
that would
call me home.
The hat of
the sun
collapsing.
The stars
tearing huge
holes in
the earth
burping
tears.
I want to
be loved
for my
indifference
throw my
notebook
throw my
sandals
off the
boat. Dripping
wet & barefoot
like a sea monster
I'd arrive.

What are
you doing.
No that
won't
work.
In the
face
of an
unimportant
universal
collapse
of all
that we
know.
I would
prefer
to begin
an under-
taking of
immense
beauty.

I would
like to
hold your
hand and
the birds
are be-
ginning
to fly.
I would
like to
kiss your
mouth &
the animals
can come
closer
now.

84

LATE MARCH

Tons of purple
out today.
Think I'll
take a
walk &
collect
some. An
old damp
shirt, dull
dog leash
nearly magenta.
The shrieks
of the
boys
when they
play
ball. Really
vaguely
lilac.
Your eyes.
Nope. While
you lay
in bed.
The purple
of separation.
Time, mauve.
Days go
by. The
boink
of the
ball as
the moments
pass in
the lazy

orchid
of Sunday
when nothing's
right,
nothing's
wrong &
I snap
on your
dark
purple
collar &
take you
home. No
reason
to cry.

Sort of an Epic

I want to worship at
the most miniscule
level. Rusty chain
link fence w/
dry red leaves
in January. I
want to put
my shiny red
cheek to its
old supports.
Nature seems
to be huffing
up from
under the
ground like
a dead woman whose
body fertilizes
the world.

Stairs lead down
from houses
into streets
long ones
with white
stripes. Stores,
people buying
food. A
kid with
a cookie
in her
mitten. Who
made the
cookie,
who made

the mitten.
Machine.
Mother.

One day
her mother
goes under
the ground.
She's eating
her cookie
& cries. I'm
like an angel
over her
shoulder
asking for
a bite.

There's a river.
Spiny reeds bursting
up from its
black & shiver
surface. Dirty
river, kids
with filth
attached
to their
backs diving
in & out
there are
only kids
in rivers
now, kids
in the
war, kids
kids kids
a new kind of
kid must
never
die. A
new kind

of
flower
bursting
up every
morning
from her
heart.

The baby
is singing. Fiddles.
Playing the
train show
tickles our
hearts
to death.
The baby
is killing
us now
as gas
fills
the schools
of Tel Aviv
or Riyadh
Baghdad or
Amman.

I wonder
where
the
children
go when
their
flowers die.
In my
belly, my
buckle,
my lover's
heart. A
baby is
swinging on

her clit
holding
a sign.
Last night
we were
lost in
the dark.
She told
me so.
I was stroking
her body
on the
beach under
the moon.
The world
was blasting
colors, I
stuck my
foot
in the
ice. She said
no! We
wandered
saw a
light   crossed
the street
& had
dinner. What's
this. There
was red
on her
hand. We
went round
the world
with death.
It was
glowing tape
like I've
said
before.

90

She told
me, folded
me up, I
embraced
her. Scooted
off to a
cozy cave
picked
a stalagmite
or two
and kissed
her tenderly
on the
head. Now
the world's
a corridor
I'm sliding
with love.
It's an
oil slick,
inevitability
an ocean
I want
or a
horse. I
love her
toes, this
wet &
gleaming
shower:

O,
one breath
two breath
grief &
going
home.

RAPE

Next time I have a show
in Boston and you sit
in the front row I'm
going to say hey were
you my boyfriend
& is this your wife?
Do you think I'm a
fucking videotape
asshole? The way
you shift in your
seats, edgy,
making like you're ready
to go. Hey is that my
mother? Hi Mom.
What if I remember
that you fucked me
too. Happy Easter,
Mom. My little
dog goes for the
frisbee chews it
up. My girlfriend
is imperious—loads
of purple. I will
lay it at her little
feet. Broken eggs.
In the chalk black
night of New York
which is frequently
day & I'm always
looking down at
those phoney 10
dollar bills or the
pink streets falling to

the river. Every
thing is continuous
nothing is lost. One
saga if you choose
not to destroy
She's not so different
as I pick it up
here as I lose it
& throw her down.
Everything's known
somehow, rising
higher each year
like a tremendous
joke that never
breaks. I may never
know why old women
are clowns, insanity's
makeup terrifies
me. I may never know
that, but the
universe speaks &
I give it change.

I never thought about
sucking my boyfriend's
cock, but I liked
it. The vague taste
of piss & sweat. Sometimes
when you eat me I
think I have a
cock & I like that
too. I recognize your
cock when you fuck
me with your whole
fucking hand, I
recognize the world
half way up your
cunt someplace in

the dark at a
party it's amazing.

What's continuous
a penny
and a loud rattling drain.

YOU

Perhaps I can sell my point of
view I thought looking up at
the trees. The white rot on
the elm reminds me of tears

       A stream
of tiny tiny green dots
covers the sidewalk,
a grey parquet
floor of octagons. Now that
I'm gone I only want to
climb up on you
cause you're it, put my
fingers on your dark brown
hills, the buses that flood
your small streets, beeping
I turned the faucet
now everything is loss

She is like some kind of daughter to the
world, prince of its gates & fences
little squirrel nuzzling up to its roots.

It's inconsequential which way I go
the breeze hits me like other
clouds of dust & "why bother"
to this sadness that
surrounds a small green
heart connected by soft fuzzy
roots to its borders that used
to stick to something but
they fell this spring, two-dimensionally
alone in the wind, and
it's silly to name the wind

too. A while ago we used
to have some gods & they
had stories that explained
the way they were. We
talk about stories
now   the way they stop &
start   say   no   no   no
you can't hurt me now
I'm not here anymore.

WALLPAPER BANKRUPTCY SALE

It doesn't help
to be grey
at moments
like this. The
early day's
cloud, sort
of a sweater
or an emblem
of my
identity,
is invisible
by night.
It's crazy
to be grey
in the
maw of
the monster,
grey in
a war.
O grey you are
neutral,
forgotten,
o grey
my sullen
weather, the
color of
storms
buildings,
minus
the names of
institutions.
It's like
sidewalks
the faces
of
the sad

It's
what you
chose
to ally
yourself
with in
a lighter,
merely
abrasive
almost
tacky
part of
the day.
Now you
are like the
rivers, the
going no
where ponds
the yawns
of late afternoon;
blood is
spilled, fortunes
lost & you've
got a clump
of wool
under your
chin for
a pillow,
eyes trained
on dawn.
Grey! You

are like
an upside
down
house &
one by
one the
lights
are going
out.

"No Poems"

It was
a little
golden
cross,
wooden
like a
ruler,
really. Wrapped
round
with pink
flowers.
Then Ann,
she put
a small
cut glass
vase of
more pink
flowers,
she leaned
across
the hole
she couldn't
quite, it
was awk-
ward
so the
monk
took the
vase and
placed
it for
her at
the foot
of the

cross,
& things
were even
moreso.
There
was a
hole in
the ground
& in it
the can.
We were
invited
to take
a hand-
ful of
dirt, earth
the name
of
our planet,
& throw it
on our
friend whose
burnt
remains
were in
the can. It
felt good,
cold, strong,
old, a
handful
of planet.
Here, I
thought &
wiped my
hand on
the brown
bandana
Duncan
brought. I
wiped the

dirt from
my hand.
My friend
was buried
under a
tree. Little
cross, stroke
of sun
hitting its
shiny gold.
We stood
in a circle,
the friends,
the monks,
brown.
One monk
lifted a
spade &
shoveled
it in, earth
to fill
the hole
& now he
was gone.
We stood.
It was
pretty
as a
picture &
he was
taking
photographs
the whine
of the
camera &
then we
stood
still. We'll
probably
come

back said
Duncan. *Huh!*
That's
what I
was just
thinking.

TRIAL BALLOON

Annie Sprinkle rolled
ink on her breasts
so that Barbara
Barg & I should
ride in a cab
back from
a radio
show in the morning
discussing language.
That, now? And
Rosie doesn't
seem to notice
him, a
friend she
usually likes
a lot, that
collie
behind
bars. & there
goes the
water, chamomile.
Words are so
funny today
behind no
sleep, especially
names.

LIFE

My sense of preservation
a gift borne to me by
my mother through
the days of
her world has
led me to
wrap bread
in plastic. Occasionally
fruit, a lime,
may sit split
in the spattered
refrigerator
door, there to
dry and get
like plastic.
But never
bread. Bread
must live.
I wish I had
a collection of
plastic things
to put all
other things
in—little bits
of food
that I
would keep
longer. Eat
later. But
not living
food like
tomatoes. No,
I mean
bread. Why

do I fear
the demise
of bread
so much
its drying
up & hardening.
Surely I
think it's
some kind
of body.
Bread's so
cheap & so
is flesh, really.
There's so much
of it daily
marching through
the streets of
my world. But
is it my world
really. I'm
just another
loaf of
bread in
shoes, marking
time. I sat
on a stoop
this afternoon
in front
of a camera
trying to
make a
glowing
impression
that would
last &
travel far.
An important
crumb. When
I read
books I

think of
my cunt. If it's
about love
of God, the
hotter I
get. I better
clean some
things up
I think
putting the
corpses of
the things
I eat
onto little
shelves. I
shut the
door &
the light
goes out.
I am God.

WE THE LIVING

As my platform I suggest
these really pretty fingers
which hold me up
a pretty cunt
splayed on the
vivid couch.
Elected to walk a dog
since you have died
& watching the day get licked
in the Park. Since you got died
Patroclus there is nothing
for me but killing. I die nighty on the couch
in the guns of the pretty fingers.
It was a round wand. A halo.
Let's start where the world
ends. We done that now—
I love you. You are dead.
Hauling the holocaust on
a leash   a halo of
nettle it seemed, I am maud
all honey with
the moon shooting through
election night &
your white hands.
The moon's an opening into something else
fuck my death now that it's happened. I
want to be truly alive. The dog grant
where they bring your leash & take
you out. Like the devil to
Jesus, all this is yours. Wind blowing
serenely
on my dog nose & the
west is not the best at all.
I want to be president of all this

shit. Ripping it open on a daily
basis. I am a woman & I
want to kill. Death to
me at the hands
of your pretty fingers, Patroclus.
Now I'm gazing into puddles.
Busses roar & the prick
of the sun is splitting
the trees on
this white white
day, January,
at the
font of
my black
black cunt

THE POET

I made myself into a poet because it was the first thing I really loved. It was an act of will. I realize that now. I was always afraid of asking for things from the devil. I would probably get them. Then I stumbled onto this idea about the purity of the heart. This is a way I could get what I want. To desire one thing, that's the idea. I knew I could do that. And I already knew what I wanted. To keep doing what I was doing, but to know that it was true. It was right for me to keep doing that, to want nothing else but that. I felt free at last. My life had become a dream. My dream. My life was the cloth of that. Days spent sharing an egg with a cat were good days. With my little red floor & white walls. & millions of men in my bed. It meant nothing. I liked alcohol. What poet didn't. I woke up in the dreaming poem of the day & made myself a hot black cup of coffee. I would begin. Soon I would want something. A cigarette. That was good. The place I bought them was far enough, a walk, good for my body, something blue for my hand. Who did I think the poet was. A talking dog. Who felt her lips with her fingertips & wrote that down. You see the page for me has terrific dimension. I can go into the white & I do. The lines are designs for something real, how much space around the slender bars I bend and shape in the name of my world. A comma is a little fish, a dash sort of a raft. When we say capitals we mean apples. German words about the same size as God. When you want to refer to that. Its comedy. Sometimes the poem wants to come home. It has a firm back, its left hand margin, sometimes it feels just fine about that. The page is the sky. My typewriter, classic, a wispy one had no spine & so my poems floated like clouds, globs of sunlessness & I marked the world free. Sensationally flat poems I know each line went from there to there was ironic as print felt that way soothed by the cruelty of wasps and was crisper than them, just a season of flat poems. Lonely the loss of rock 'n roll. It was receding. My poems were flat. A woman made me ache, I was love on the page not yet I had always felt like a brick shit house. I was the poem. The incident in the afternoon the folded sheet, I was the mouth the sounds emitted from I was the pipes of god, me this structure this eternity. Enter it. The oldest dream I remember an important one was about a train in the night going to Germany & I must get on & save myself. Once in a while I say be full, and it is, be slow, oh tear holes in me as the day dies. I have truly become my poems, but do note the sculpture of others, their obliviousness, like architects leaving crumbs. It is not lost my century, thanks to us. We are the liars & thieves, we are the women we are the women I am full of holes because you are. I am the only saintly man in town. Don't be afraid to be feminine. A girl on a rowboat, full of holes. She saw words shooting through.

TO THE CLASS OF '92

You all look great
I'm sorry it's raining today
but sunny days are kind
of simple minded. A nice
grey day for the class of
'92, I mean how could it
be any other way. And
look at the world we're
releasing you into. Are
you sure you want to
go. I definitely didn't
want to leave college
when I was in school.
I didn't even like the
school I went to
but do you think that
made a lot of difference?
I was quaking. I wanted
to keep making sandwiches
in my mother's house &
taking the bus in & then
the train. I didn't like
doing it, but I didn't
want it to end ever.
It's sort of like youth
& that's why you are.
& that's why you look
great. You're all so
fucking radiant that
even on a rainy day
you cut right through
& I feel moved. I've
got to warn you
this is not going to be a short

speech. I am not windy,
but I am certainly not
brief. I think you asked
me to speak at your
graduation because you
like my campaign &
you want me to win.
Well I want you to win
too. If we can't all
become president of
the united states then
I think no one
should. Do you know
what I mean? Spiritually
at least. When I went
to college everyone was
very spiritual. I mean
not at my little commuter
U. but certainly at a
school like this. Certainly
the class of '71 had
a mind for those
things. Very few wore
caps & gowns anywhere
& actually most people
didn't go to graduation
Ceremony = tedium &
we wanted no part
of that. We wanted
to be free. How
many of you
want to be free
today. It doesn't
make sense. Wanting
that is like wanting
nothing. And if everyone
can't be free why
should anyone. I don't
want to be president
of the united states

so I can free people.
Or, so I can free my
ambitions, unleash
my will upon America.
Let Mr. Perot do that.
Freedom is ineffable.
Can we hold that spot
for a moment. Because I
think you're incredibly
free here, at this moment
perched on this maybe
meaningful precipice
of life. And I mean
that "maybe" with
all my heart. I was
really delighted when
I was asked to speak
here today. Because
this is such a good
school. Some of
you come from rich
families & it was no
sacrifice for them
to send you here
& some of you
are on scholarships & loans, maybe
most of you, right. So you'll
never forget this school. But
it's a nice place, very beautiful
& protected—I kind of envy
you and I feel obliged by
all of these things—my envy
my delight & even my sense
of duty to kind of underline
the meaning of this moment
when you are leaving school.
It seems very short to me
now. The time you spent
here, 4 years goes very
fast so perhaps what you'll

be saying goodbye to when
you leave here is slow
time. (Long silence.) Wasn't
that hell? Something in
me gets de-railed mentally,
it's always been so. I
make most of my living
as a public speaker, this
is what I do & yet I
freeze up like a deer in
the light of your attention &
like something that's bound
to be killed by the swerve
of your attention I've
begun to relish it. Because
it's so slow before you
die. Think of it this
way—you're dying now.
I just knew I'd say the
wrong thing. People are dying now.
Maybe it's you. How different you'd
look at today if it was about
your death. How cruel of us to
come & watch. To make our
speeches to honor you. To see
you sitting here in tears on this
rainy day. There's something really
interesting about that. You didn't
ask for the normal speaker &
you won't get a normal speech.
Hillary Clinton gets paid
more than me for lying
to you. So does Barbara
Bush. Graduation day is
meaningless. I respect you all a lot
more than us, your parents'
generation. Twenty years
ago with our reverence for nothing.
You are clinging to the forms that
are handed to you, but you know

they are nothing. Isn't that true.
This is not the fifties. You
don't believe in those gowns.
After all of us have finished
talking the band will strike
up a song you have never heard
before & you will be expected
to sing. But you can't. The
words are gone, you wish you
could sing them but the death
of forms is all around you.
You are the most human class
of all. You have invited me
to speak today because I
love you. It's not what
you expected from a political candidate
but I didn't expect to get asked
to speak at the end of the world.
Think of yourselves as chosen.
It's true in a way. You could
be holding a gun, you could be dying
racked by coughs with so many tubes,
you could be tired of dying like that.
It happens to some people. People
you know. There are women
squeezing babies out of their
loins, such a moment &
the lights go out. He never
knew what happened. She didn't
know what hit her. Some of you
have watched a parent die. As
they inch out of your world
you step up to the diving board
of life, imagine it, a broad
one for all of you. In your
little red cloaks, the candidates,
all ready to walk out into
the world to change it. To
what! It's much too
late. I'd like my check.

I've got to go. Rodney
King says we're stuck
here. Are we? Need each other
as much as you can bear.
Everywhere you go in the
world.

WARRIOR

Sensation of the supermarket
I can go this far
you're curling & wild
almost dying in the car ten seconds
out of water, you don't travel
well. Your smell is not sweet
but itchy, like sex in the woods
rarely does one purchase
such a smell. Usually stumbled
on, remembered. So while you're almost
vanishing, I'll say we were spontaneous
How did such white meet such fuchsia
& then hot pink. A smattering
of intelligent antennae
a scribble of brains
amidst the curly blossoms
and the thin slim pods
future flowers, it's clear
you've got a way to go. Anyone can
look at you real fast & say
she's everything. I see cactus,
I feel thorny prickles, no one
knew your name, no one in the fruit
stand at 9 & 9G. I rode home
with your flavors on my lap.
& I say this for wildness
even as it's dying
it's very very powerful

AUTHENTICITY

There's pivotal moments
in bouncing time.
My friend goes racing
across the green
bright red car takes
a corner and behind
the right hand of
this green tree looms
a water tower—the only
religion a small town
knows. I don't
have your ball
I'm sorry to
say. In light
rain a white haired
woman steps off
a bus, it's raining
harder & I almost
can't write, the
dog's brown butt
is bouncing
through tear
drops. Why
the rain?
Cause the 19th century's
gone. I saw
the empty train
tracks at Barrytown
the prettiest little
station you ever
did see. All
across Canada
more of the
same and

under the convenient
roof in a
playground we
rest & more
of the same the
roar of the
rain is a blast
from the past. Goodbye
19th century—trash
barrels in Barrytown
filled to the gills
Germany trying to
transport its
shit to France
& vice versa. You
wept about this
playground one
night, the end
of your childhood.
& I didn't need
to cry about any
thing at all
because I
have nature.
You tried to
show me something
beautiful you did
& nature sounds
like a bowling
alley right
now. What
is coming down
the lane for
us. A spotted
deer, peanut
butter colored
crossed our
path, it passed
& I felt like
my life had

been folded
in half
I'm free now
I've killed
a deer,
had deer
dreams, raced
to the ocean
holding its
horns, &
now I have
spared the
creature. You
brought me
this. Your desire
for a squirrel
is stronger
than the
part that
wants to
stay dry
we're driving
through colleges
now that
fail to move
me in the
manor that
playgrounds do.
You can buy
a piece of
the nineteenth
century if you're
really rich.
God, they
would turn
around & buy
something for
everyone,
those robber
barons, but

I would
settle for
a cigarette.
I go to
Bark &
I major
in ball. So
many things
were sort of
purplish red, those
flowers, wavering
in front of
a corrugated
wall. It
made them
speak to
me as many
& single. I
was moved &
we were driving
through the
20th century
then. So many birds
forced from
the top of
a dark
green tree
paint-by-numbers
very very dark
it was a
high pressure
situation. Starling,
how contrived
of them to
name the
girl that
way like
a bird that
fascinated
my dog. It's

an incredible
industry of
colors. This little
town gives
you space to
own them
all. Owning
in the sense
of the 21st
century. Not
putting a gate
around all
this space or
driving through
but having a
vision that's
real & fake
soft footsteps
semi-metallic
rain, millions
& millions
of singers
when one
leaf falls
you need
not hope
for another
one

SAPPHO'S BOAT (1982)

TUESDAY BRIGHTNESS

We had a fight so
We didn't fuck at night.
The unemployment office was a series
Of lines and I signed up.
And at home I ate Philadelphia cream cheese,
Thomas' english muffins.
Color xeroxed *Catholic Comics*.
Sent to Katz. "Isn't color xerox a miracle, Steve?"
Post Office. Cobbler's.
Big library where read Sappho.
Holes and all. Feel the wind
Shifting through. Aeolics.
Shiver when Sappho speaks of her
Heart Beat. It
Pounding down through the ages.
Old adrenaline, gives me a rush.
And morning sex was nice. In
morning light. Day blast-off.
Rusharound. Through the lightness.
Nightness come cover me. Let's
Go around again.

"ROMANTIC PAIN"

And in the first bar
the woman next to me said, "
How would you like to be introduced
to a couple of muscle-bound ..."
Then she talked about when she
had been chef, "Moist juicy
salad with russian dressing"
I gulped my bourbon & walked
out the door.
The second bar was all women.
Bartender, a chubby Diane Keaton.
Woman to my left, also
in the bar business. Woman
to my right, passed out.
I sipped my bourbon and listened
          to the jukebox.

I'd been asleep all day. I wanted to
be tired again. I looked up
and the sky was very dark.
I must see morning. I must
get off my ass, walk
and get tired.

Passed Canal Street. Walked through the plaza
of the criminal courts. Lit a cigarette
near a potted tree on Chambers Street.
World Trade towers   immense quiet and barely
lit. Past the giant post office,
patriotic trucks coming in and out of the garage.
Retreat to the womb. A pregnant silence.
Rounding the corner, catholic relief place,
free lunches for old sailors. I
decide to ride the escalator

like I never do ... up into the
ferry building. A last resort.
People sacked out on wooden benches.
Strange ladies room with door
wide open so everyone watches you look at
             yourself. No one watches.
All crashed out on benches. I re-assemble
a red-stained newspaper. Get askance
stares like I'm a young bag-lady.
I looked pasty in the bathroom.
Eyes like raccoons. My hair's screwed up.
My jacket looks "boxy."

The sign that says NEXT BOAT
goes green. We herd on,
rumpled, tobacco-mouthed, the black guy
calling the white woman with the little dog
"Weird"   "a weird bitch"
He looks to me. Looks at me.
I try to tell him it's OK,
I am a weird bitch. The boat smells of
donuts and is filled with cops,
conductors, strange people coming home
from strange nights. I go in the
ladies room & see the woman
with the little dog. She plucks a
Winston from her pack. And an
oriental woman. Terribly neat. I
want to look at myself in the mirror
but I look so shitty I don't want
to expose my third-rate vanity. The
other two of us light a cigarette.
Three women at different angles
smoking cigarettes. We each sneak
peeks at ourselves in the mirror.
Push this piece of hair. Move
that collar   Inspect that eyelash.
          I can see us from overhead
and call the configuration "Feminism."

And the boat pulls out. I am brave
I am Hart Crane, I push the
    brown door aside and stand out on
        the deck. This is what I
came here for. The "me" movie,
    me on the deck in slight rain at
      5AM looking at the Statue of Liberty
swathed in mist. I want to wave.
I always want to wave at her.

It's kind of cold and I think of
    various deaths in my family,
      how I'd go to see various gravestones
trying to exert some sorrow. Trying to
    create the sorrowful setting as
this one is "romantic pain," me alone in the
    rain on a boat and it's cold
      and I want a cigarette.
I huddle under the overhanging upper deck
    trying to light one. A cop comes
      by & I stealthily turn,
the wind picks my pack from my hands
    and I chase it and it scares me
me running on this deck &
    I think how desperate I was
    looking and I think the
    cop thinks now that I'm
going to jump & I sit on the
    orange boat-bench
thinking what a fucked up reason for
   suicide that would be,
    just living up to some cop's anticipation.
      Ha! I chuckle,
      my kind of death

and I head downstairs
  where the scum are allowed to
smoke, the windows thick
    with grime, the smell of
  decades of sour-mouthed

                smokers   and I smoke.
                    And I watch Staten Island
approach.
                        Feeling the fool
            I make a U-turn in the
                hallway & look for the entrance
                    to the New York ferry.

                    I hope the crew is different.
                    I check the name of the boat but
                        it doesn't matter. I didn't
notice the other boat's name.

                    I make my perfunctory
            tour of the deck. I feel
        like Hart Crane. The wind smacks my
            hair, washes it over my cheeks &
                    I wish I could cry.
        The boat feels right this time.

                    Downstairs to smoke.
        I always smoke. And it's crowded
                this time. Morning people,
        foggy like night people but cleaner.
            Clean shirts, nylons, heels
            people drinking coffee as they
            smoke their cigarettes. The
                fat man over there,
                    he keeps winking at me.
                I think, thinking I have no subway
                    money, "For 50 cents I'll give
                    give you something to wink
                        at."

All the way home
            through Chinatown, through
            the Bowery, back in the
    business section, the awakening city,
            sitting on the bench across
                the street from
            the brand new FAMILY COURT

building,

I keep looking for it, that wonderful
10, the 20 dollar bill
waiting for me, lying on the
ground. I keep my head
down all the way home. My feet
hurt. And I missed the
dawn. The
goddamn dawn, Said Hart Crane.

PTOLEMY

September and the shit in the streets is
        turning colors
    skipping out in the rain to buy
            more beer   resuming conversation
    Michael   "the ideal & the real"
            real being the sex act
        ideal the 10 minutes prior
            hold the image
        waiting for the other
                to get a nice vision.

Or I thought the ideal was the idea of astral
    projection compared to the physical
            sensation of
        flying in my dreams. I'm never
    tempted to jot down a line
                and the feeling of erupting
                    poem
            in my solar plexus is simply that
                a poem coming
            & of course I'm too busy to
                    fly.

I hate to acquaint you with my boredom.
    Windows full of untouched wilderness
        like gradeschool painting
    music blowing through my apartment
        as I am surely lying prone.
    The idea of the monad   the jot
            being a dream of the
                alchemists.
        Final point of white light
        being the reality of late
    night teevee. I'm touched

by the optimism of little girls
who took "Joan" as their
confirmation name. Then
the mild slap delivered
by the aging Cardinal
... disappointment
and the short hair-
cut all for naught. But the
adventurous dive from the tower! Original
falling dream
flying upwards in my head
like a buddhist
holding back sperm.
The hard smack to the ground.
Joni Mitchell
Emma Goldman
Simone de Beauvoir and
her sexual frustrations.
Free-loving Sartre.
Down the alley comes the
undoubting
ball. Strikes are
overwhelming compared
to the equanimity of
"spares."
The pairs in my life I
can't swim through.
Obvious ones like night and day
female and male   yesterday and tomorrow
the ongoing now slipping
by like a thief.   Robbery as
an incredible philosophy.
If I could rip off the
moment   run chuckling
to the stars.   Call a
constellation after
me.
I lean
miles above
my head

and yet
would like to
smoke. Provoke
a few clouds
to hide
beyond. Beyonder.

So Realism

for Michael Lally

Poem in my pocket
    crossing the street
sky looks great
      unreal   so so
        painted I guess
      heraldic blue w/ clouds underlined
            in tacky silver   so deco
      my poem packed up in squares
            quadrants
        shit sounds like a heart
and me eight hours battling on
        bet I won't even show you
        this one
only got to offer fabulous sex
          love poems
    & O I don't know   jokes too
        I suppose
        but why's it so bad
why's it always so bad
         never artificial & pretty
        like that day.

La Vita Nuova

            Love is an assumption
that is my argument
        rudely transposing me
        as a certain process
            or in relationship to sanity
    or I suppose this is an argument
                        between the body &
        the soul
                        whether the chicken hatches
        the egg.
    Alone in my soul
            or through the bodies of others
                    which confuse
                    & disarm
            in a really provocative manner.
                        O
        what financial disaster
    to lie among sheep
    propose that all men are sheep
                    all women.
        Plato has me hot in drag
                and they're all brilliant
            perceptions. Who amongst
                me is really getting off? Trans-
    positions rudely transposing me.
        In my argument I am amused.
                        I'd really like to tell
        you of my love. But
    in describing I would name,
                lose
        my love in attempts
                        to praise.
                You must know I'm talking to you.
    The absolutely horrible

                    cotillion of my thoughts.
          I'd like to get really stoned
    and revise everything I've ever done.
                    Leaning
          against the refrigerator
    thinking I would kill to be
                    in bed with you right
                    now.
                    I get up.
          Turn down my hamburger, re-establishing
    myself
                    into a reading at the
                    Gotham, a man next to me
    comments, "It's amazing
          how Irish Catholics
    are so uncomfortable inside
                    of their bodies ..."
          I smile knowingly

                    Bernadette Devlin crossing
                    the border
                    I get up again to put cheese on
                    my burger
                    theorizing of poems based
          on appetite, the time elapsed
                    proceeding on the multitudes
          of varying angles
                    separate climes ...
    Am I not inside my life?
          Is my life the many places I can be
                    alive in & not get nostalgic
                    about?
          Is man alone in the Universe?
          What about me? I'm
                    replacing a lightbulb
          and thinking about you.
          I'm a phoney. The illusion of love
                    is no substitute
                              for the actual

experience of being a carpenter
which I have never
ever considered being.

SAILAWAY

Listen
 I will chase you to
  to the ends of the
   earth
    It's so heavy
   I'm embarrassed
     by my emotion
   its sheer scare
     quality

I know it
   is completely too much
    it's how you play
     which drives me
      makes me
        follow through
    my love
       of storm
        breeze
       my uneasy boat.

138

POEM ON THE PROFESSION

Language interests me
more than life
I just want to see where it goes—
explaining tonight I get
on a train enter a big party
dance go make love with you
go mail a letter tomorrow
go invent cigarettes.
Stop I want to turn the wheel!
so slightly to the right
examine evening through late-day
or morning glimpses—
Um apologetically in the rush

of color teevee, hot poem
by her who writes songs
enhances action
in the embrace of a tall cowboy
I think I see snow
"Alive burden"
I think we both are looking in
the Window.

APRIL

Birds tweeting
    red green blue laundry flustering
        on a line
            springtime
    light
    around five o'clock
come stroke me softly I would suggest
        O forget it
      I'm just another bird
              as blue seeps between build-
ings

    I'm enamored of branches
   the billion-fingered tree
          "seasonal amazing"
   the year always gets
             young again
you could refuse
       and it keeps doing it
   How could I refuse your soft fingers
         Spring?
        Or why do I talk to you at all
        Such a fool for the
    annual come-on.

   I know you see my love as
        artificial
         something that keeps covering
     as I'm blundering
      toward
        you.   You're right,
    I'm all talk   my truest
lover
    I hug it in my sleep

I should learn
    a more irregular love
                  there's no lying
    when it comes to green
  bursting
    all around.

    What I really want
  is to stay here in Spring
    soft and
          breezy
    tiny infatuation in
    the back
  of my mind   catch
a glance at someone beautiful
    "sweet shiver"
  a soft day's passing
    just before
          twilight
and the wonderful wonderful birds
              clustering
  along the
    lowering lights.

EXPLODING THE SPRING MYSTIQUE

Good Morning, World! Captain Eileen here
At her little morning desk
Dying to tell you at the crack of dawn
How dearly she hates it
How Spring truly sucks.

Here we have it outside my morning window
Birds twittering, buds newly greening on perky branches
       "Tweet," another fucking bird.

And I had to go through a whole night to get here.
That's the part that's really hard to swallow.
I had to lie awake for hours thinking of how I hate just about
Every man, woman and child who walks the face of this earth
Myself included, I find self-hate extremely motivating

I thought of everyone I've ever fucked or wanted to and
Thought how unrewarding it was. "Can't take it with you!"
Like they say.
I thought of the conversations I've had.
Nearly the mystery was unravelled in 1962.
Then in 64, 67, 72, 73 and 74. And those were the transcendent
Conversations. Not to mention the warm friendly variety, or
The pitiful confessional motif. Both of you
Pour out your sorrows and feel instantly better.
"And I thought I was fucked up!" each thinks.

I thought of my dreams of becoming a great poet & then I
      thought of
My poet friends who dream no differently. I thought of my
Poet friends and how they have no right to live within
The revolting egocentric realities uniquely expressed in
Syntax all their own and then they print their own poems
In their own little magazines.

142

Was it Marlon Brando who said, "Looking up the asshole
    of death."
Anyhow, by 35 most poets either can't do it anymore
Or have ruined their lives or the lives of others or have
Simply realized that all of it was a farce.
Suddenly struck at 35 by the genuinely mediocre fact of your
    life
Which previously stood as a backdrop to the cosmos or
    culture
And now ... Har, Har, Middle-Aged Poet!
Joke's on you. Broke and not very good-looking.

Though I don't plan to stop at this moment.
Sure, I hate my friends and they hate me and there's no one
    around to
Fuck except the ones who won't fuck me and they like to
    torture me
And I like it—my poems keep getting better and better.
But the fact is
If I am no longer a poet, then I will have to face being a
    useless and
Mediocre human being now, rather than when I'm 35, as is
    the norm
35 will be terrifying.
A) Unless dead or raving mad or abandoned with a large
    shopping bag
And a pint of Wild Irish Rose, I will be B) teaching a
    work-shop
or C) penning a villanelle, as one poet puts it, or
D) just taking a shit and suddenly the joke will be swarming
    all
Around me, a nettle of fears and doubts, cold icy sweat,
    perhaps
I'll be standing on a stage reading a fucking sonnet and
Whomp!   "Your life is meaningless! This is the last
    message!"

"What, What ..." I'll mutter, swinging my arms around
    spastically
But I know what it means: "You blew it, Baby   It was a joke."

143

So I go home to my lover (If I'm that fucking lucky when I'm
35 … Why should it start then? But listen, this is the
    clincher …)

I go home to my lover, who's of course in her early 20s
A Younger Poet. There's a note on my pillow
Sorry, Honey, you peaked.
Arrrgh! I shriek at the heavens.
All those years I chortled at men: Ha! You guys are done in
At 18. Your "prime." We women don't peak until 35.
I collapse on my bed, a sexual and artistic homicide.
Though still breathing, and it is Spring.

ANGEL PUNK

What I really like to do is go home
and wipe the world off my face
    a silken robe and a quick pome.
5 o'clock is gorgeous with its deepening blues and
    flash of sky blue pink

    I'm so alarmed by my procrastination
    I've lost my memory   I'm unable to paint.

Where would you like to take me?

    I'm Annie Oakley
    I love your shirt I confess to his pockets
or someone ties me up in scarves and we tear off
    to join the gypsies.

Pennies fascinating, I pick them up all day
between bird glimpses
    I feel tamed

    by benevolence sloth and ambiguity.

Really I'm sort of lying around waiting for Joan of Arc
    in her old white Porsche
      bottle of Remy
    I have strictly monetary dreams.
In real life of course I'm totally into kindness

    it's sort of the hammock of ambition.

    I persist in renaming you over a bowl of black
             bean soup
    symptomatically bored by the present and
    I like it better when I write your name

all over bathrooms erasing and laughing
—Angel Punk! The Fourth of July comes
and so do we. I see masturbation go down the drain

and my clean well-lit life.

MADELINE REVENGE

It's such a bust to call this an occupation
You hand me a peach or a pear
And criticize the peach as I bite into it.
Somehow being so blammed down
A pleasure, or what brings me closer
To the sweetness that the truly mad contain.

I hate you like I hated nuns.
You don't have to stop
Somehow you've got this kind of permission

Dominance floods the room with its dark wings
I either stand up and screech like a chicken

Or what brings me nearer is this separation
Here, where I can slither my feelings
Across sheer ice.

Till Death Do Us Part

for Anne McDonough

was filled by RD Laing
Cream and if
only I could get on that bus
and go away.
Love never sang nor ever
sometimes I felt quite mad.

But often I was excited
there were things I thought
were everything   But of course
they weren't everything.

But everything wasn't something
I let go of   Shapeless
but imploring
I picked up pricks & books
no, books & pricks.

MY RAMPANT MUSE, FOR HER

Tuesday night   reading *For Love* on
my bed. Or writing *For Love*
  poem is wishing
     when I stop waiting. One thousand times

I've read & wrote *For Love*
    wear my sneakers, drink
  my bourbon,
        be 28 in spite of me

     in mirrors, Christ!
   I look fucking *old*

       What does the evening
mean? I could fall for lamp-light,
   radio-song,
  "the oval shaped frame of which
  he was particularly fond ...

      For Love I would dream
when my schemes fall through, Man,
   could that little girl dance! *For Love* I will read
it 10,000 times   for my tomboy cousin Jean Marie,
    for radio song, *For Love*
I would not pity me, my 28, sneakers, bourbon
              the unseen
   future of my communications, and   the lamp-
   light, Her, she holds me here, so
   rampantly
   in her evening beauty.

Whax 'n Wayne

for Barbara

THE stars were glowing tonight
like all the paranoia in the universe

The air was chill
though it's early March
but that makes sense

Doesn't it, Love, Doesn't it?
and a five-dollar bill
is cold upon my ass, my blood is cold,
footsteps shattering the stairs
up to my level
then past it.
I only want a place on the line, I don't
want it to stop with me or start
with me, really I don't want it to know I'm here
at all, I only love what finds me invisible
and touches me deeply. Cold does that
and that's how I love the vanishing winter. I used to count
breaths in the night, one night I counted the church-bells
    falling
into a marsh and growing silent. It was two days before I dis-
covered boys, and tonight is two days after. I feel like
a woolen sock on the line, rippling, the season doesn't care
about me and I'm using it without its permission.
It's the new god, the one that doesn't know about me at all,
who misses me in movies, restaurants, who doesn't count my
wheels spinning—who could count silence? *that's the one I love.*
Loneliness sharpens into something sweeter, my sadnesses
    sharpening
themselves, christian thorns, You Bet! Apples bananas
    particularness

150

which doesn't exist at all is a bird too big for churches so
churches grow as good as *movies, restaurants*   silence is
      running
tonight to get hot coffee, to smoke, to breathe
everyone is going home to someplace, me too, love creates
      loneliness,
I never knew that before.

Television is what the night eats.
I eat some soup, some bread, old black coffee reheated like
      favorite
shoes, you're like a fireplace I just want to be around.
Five bucks chill upon the ass, I think I'll buy the morning
      and some
of the afternoon. O pink tulip, o other pink tulip, *2 yellows*,
the length of this room, peaceful cats, outside it's cold,
damn it whatever happened to Spring? She comes before the
      other,
don't you know, you know, Primavera—*get it, get it,* get it?
I can stand in back of anyone I want, man or woman and
      anyone
who wants to stand in back of me is welcome, in fact they
      can stand in
front of me if they know how to do it, *do you get it?*
I think we are an army of trees. When I tripped
I only wanted to sit down everything was moving so much,
catholic poets only pray, no matter what they say
if I'm really vain I could propose to jump back into the pool,
just like it was a room, just like I'm not just a stupid feather
      on
an immense wing, Love's taught me a loneliness I never
      imagined.
This side of the hallways, umm I don't know ... *smokier?* I
      always
thought I really loved Dante but now I know what he meant.
Mark says 9 represents chaos,
Dante thought 9 was the music of the spheres.
Mark is a musician and if you could draw a line between
      those two guys
I would call it history, hang a sock or two like me.

Affluence is holding out a dollar and receiving exactly what
     you want,
I call that economics, when I say "television" you know exactly
what I mean, I call that a modern idea, a word, "television,"
get it? Let's do it again: "time," Take the word breast,
take tit, what gets erotic is which word you prefer, what gets
warm is speechless … the cold things are easy to enumerate:
stars, paranoia, ideas under blankets
kiss my teeth. If a woman wakes up remembering her dreams
and she tells her lover and she doesn't lie at all
and the next night the lover dreams something entirely
     different
and all day both lovers think about each other's dreams
and go and have different dreams the next night
and they just enjoy telling the dreams each morning
with their coffee. If a cat nibbles on flowers
I lift it off the table and make it stop because it is ugly.
Dreams are some kind of flowers and when I pour coffee into
     my cup
this morning, for example, and I feed the cats this stuff I
     wouldn't
eat, I go to the bank, drink some orange juice at Bini-bons.
Stuff with real pieces of orange in it. I drink a real big glass
of the stuff. The *New York Post* has one article about "peace,"
one about "terrorism." A guy in Weehawken is watching
The Ten Commandments on "television"   *Boom*
a cuban storefront explodes while Moses is receiving the
     tablets.
Let's call that channel religion. Or science fiction.
Then the *New York Post* has an article about SHAPING UP.
I'm always thinking about that and I suppose my body reforms
accordingly. Lover, lover, here's a flower.
It doesn't think, It's like my mother.
I wasn't interested in the newspaper
it was just something I needed to hold. All the time I have
     dreams
that could have happened. "No more orange juice" or
     someone turns
to me and speaks a line I just wrote and I wonder if they
read a poem of mine lying on my desk or am I dreaming or,

152

I don't know, maybe there's different flowers in the vase
from when I fell asleep—well I don't live alone so there's no
reason to be surprised that different flowers are in the same
    vase.
When I dream I dream nothing extraordinary. That's what
    I'm
trying to say. If something's broken maybe the cat did it.
The wooden counter at Bini-bons is more interesting
than the newspaper but if I sat here reading the counter
I'd look like an asshole. Reading a little bit
from each article I read like a bird.
I used to read like a horse until I went to college.
I felt all that knowledge coming at me through a screen.
Television fills the silence, I pay my check and leave a tip.
"The word is at the end; it's the thing's dead body." Words
of the Baby Bertolt Brecht. O—please pick up your grilled
tomato and cheese—please *eat* it. I didn't meant what I
said. All week long I've seen nothing but Lilacs.
Up and down Lexington Avenue, St. Marks Place, through
windows of classy restaurants. But there's nothing
classy about lilacs; they used to line the trees on the street
where I lived. Children in spring bringing home big
armfuls, marching up twilit spring nights carrying
purple lilacs home to mothers waiting on screened porches.
Nineteenth century flower book says *Lilac*—Purple,
first emotions of love. Surprised me, I expected
death, something melancholic and fading. I am so taken
by these flowers these days. Days expanding and shrinking
so I am sure I am no form at all. Just your eyes and
my stupidity. Some people are so sure they aren't loved
they'll throw themselves to the task of being hateful. If
only I could buy some Lilacs on a full moon night and run
here panting and wild. Be something perfect that doesn't
count and change. But I grew up where lilacs were free,
didn't everyone? So I'll just watch them all spring
in restaurants and flower shops … full and soft
as the lights go down, the moon comes up and another
season starts shouldering in. But the purple lilacs
are the most beautiful and I will always love you.

YELLOW TULIPS

I was walking along the sidewalk
in all the daily pain
& miserable faces & awful air.
Up above in a flower box
were yellow tulips, too real
to be real, so big
and sexual-looking in
that funny way flowers
always are. I guess
they were like heads
poking in from another
world. How do you
like Wednesday, you
beautiful things?

NEW YORK TULIPS

Then a group of you
found singing in a park
around a stupid old historical statue
Some tulips are completely
red, and some are terribly yellow.
Then the others shaded by both
maybe less clearly this or that.
But the mixed tulips
I love for their compassion.
They soften the blows
of this & that
I find them very beautiful.

JOAN

Today, May 30th, Joan
of Arc was burned.
She was 19 and
when she died
a man saw white doves
fly from her mouth.

Joan was born in 1412
between Lorraine
and Champagne. Joan
was raised on legends.
Merlin said France would be
lost by a woman and saved
by a virgin. Joan was
not an adventurous girl, not
a tomboy, but very dreamy,
good, stay-at-home,
the baby of the family.
Joan never got her period.

She heard these voices
in the bells, she saw angels
in colored glass. She believed
the sun moved around
the earth because that's
what she saw. She believed
God wanted Charles VII
to be King of France
because that's what Michael,
Catherine & Margaret told
her when she listened to
the bells. Her father
said he'd drown her
if she didn't stop this

nonsense.

She was 19 years old
when they burned her body in the middle of town
while she was still alive. A white dove
came out of her mouth as she died.
Five hundred and forty-eight years ago today.
A dove leaped right out of her mouth.

JUNE-STONES

Can't you feel the … Quick
    a breeze hits the leaves   excitable
then down & smooth   curious
White Cat hops to the sill
    "She once was …

    an imitation carnation, Pink
peeks from a cheap cut-glass
    vase, another
 another softer breeze, "that
    was a small one
but very nice"

It's like Nature comes in, here it goes
    but for one moment,
      babbling, But, But,
You're so beautiful, really,
    and a necklace
      just a string of them
a string of tiny shiny ones.

6/18

UNLEASHED

Candida took me to Fiorucci on Friday.
She encouraged me to buy the poster of the woman
I fell in love with. She is blondish, stepping
Out of the ocean with a very knowing boyish
Look in her eye, lovely thin arms, nice breasts
And her mid-section is flat tanned and softly
Muscular. I just couldn't buy a poster
Of a woman in Fiorucci—"Lookit the big dyke buyin
A poster of a chick." She's on my wall right now,
Always stepping out of the ocean and I like her
Very much. Candida just said "Buy it."
Even Barbara after a while admitted she was okay.
We sat on the couch sipping Lite beer discussing
The woman's body and I wonder if she drinks beer.
I'll meet her some night in Amsterdam. She'll have
These big boots on and she'll be sipping a Heinekens.
I'll remind her of the poster and she'll say: "Oh that."
Barbara came visiting New York two years ago and I
Came in smoking a cigar and that's how she remembers
Me. I saw this woman with beautiful sad eyes
In Rose's loft. She puts up posters on the wall of
Veiled women from Iran, and then she writes
Lesbian Nation on the kitchen wall and she changes everything.
Barbara comes in the door in a pure white teeshirt and
Brand new Lees. "He told me to come back at ten." "I'm
Writing a poem." "Go ahead." Apples banana and orange
In the bowl left over from lunch. Barbara's nipples standing
Up in her white teeshirt—some guy on twenty-third street
Said "I like your titties" to Barbara and I kicked him
In the leg. I think I scared myself more than him.
Barbara's lying on the bed reading a book. I don't
Know where this is going at all, getting wider and wider.
I'm running into the next room in the bar in Amsterdam:
"Barbara, she's here, the Fiorucci woman … Barbara, Barbara."

159

LORNA & VICKI

Inside the White House lives the President
of the United States and the First Lady lives
with him. It makes me think about history:
amazing that anyone could,
or would want to live in there
especially to live with a guy who lives
in there. To live with some children, too.
Lesbian mums are shaking in the breeze
or to really tell the truth
this Smith-Corona is shaking the table
is shaking the grey stone mug that holds
the lavender mums so they shake.
I was riding down 5th Avenue yesterday and
the jostling vehicle started getting me off
and I started pressing my finger
against the seam of my jeans between my
legs—it got even better,
but then I thought "Oh Eileen, let nature
take its course. I've had orgasms sitting
at the back of the bus—on the far
left, right over the motor. And pedalling
up a hill on a hot summer day I was nearly knocked
off my bicycle by one but I was young
and I thought it was a religious experience.
Masturbation will always be my favorite
form of sex, though if I was a tree
I'd just stand there in the breeze.

My mother used to spend a lot of her summer
evenings trying to cajole me
into doing the dishes. Eventually she'd do
this thing called "getting them started"—
or "letting them soak." I couldn't stand it.

The same way I can't stand this Smith-Corona
growling or humming while I'm looking for
a word. I like to do my waiting in silence—
I don't mind that pup yapping out my window
she's not even slightly mindful of my mums
or my mother or you napping on the couch
or… Soaking dishes irritated my abandon.
Despite the fact I'm putting it off,
something's getting done. Each moment the job
gets a little easier and by the time
I slide my hands into the water and pull
out a plate: "Your idea was a good one, Mom.
Several hours of soaking have certainly loosened
up the food particles clinging to this evening's
dishes. I'm sure these'll be done in a jiff
thanks to you." Or water,
but that's the point. And sun is much the same.
If you put a couple of tea bags in a quart jar
of water and set the whole mess on your fire-escape
you wind up with something called Sun Tea.
Just think about it. Add some lemons.
It makes me wonder what wind can do—
while you're not even looking. Apparently
it jostles the leaves and petals too
—it's nature's favorite form of sex I bet. Turning
rain into a storm, knocking the angles of rain-
drops around like pool balls. Silently
though. Not the storm but the movement.
Movement is pretty quiet as long as it's not work.
I guess it was Thursday morning during a tropical
storm called David that I put on this tarp-type
poncho and went up on the roof
to see a lunar eclipse. Naturally the storm
had masked the event—the sky was a smudged
peach but loaded somehow—it actually felt magnetic.
The moon doing this thing you couldn't see,
well I was standing on my roof inside magic
a very mad and pleased Druidical woman
I wanted to pray to somebody or something,

wind or rain or downstairs in the warmth
when I took my clothes off and got
back in bed and fell asleep.

A WOMAN LIKE ME

for Rose Lesniak

Wanna hear something really funny?
The urge to write a poem
That looks like this:
Is gone.
Behold the blank napkin on the bar
My Love.
O!
This bartender named Marilyn
Has just neatly placed
Six candles in six rocks glasses.
She is not a priest
As the good pope tells us
There are no woman priests.
Ah! Thank God who isn't
Listening to women.
Ostracizing us
Is endearingly political
& it's time for *the revolution.*
Nothing very newsy
Just the toppling of the patriarchy
The shooting of the pope in
Chicago or Washington
By a lesbian.
A lesbian like me.
Here we have the reason
Why all the napkins are Pretty & Pure.
There's this lunatic with a gun
Running loose
& she's not inclined
to sit on a napkin.
& here she goes reminiscing:
I had a date & I wore a dress

in *1969*
& this guy & I
Walked down to the Charles
& so I could sit down
He unfolded his handkerchief
& placed it on the grass
So I could sit down with
My dress & my little heels &
Really a little *ribbon*
Tying part of my long-hair
Back
& I just looked at him &
I looked at the napkin
& all the World Turned inside my
Stomach
& I place my ass on that napkin
& my eyes crossed & I looked
At the big buildings
Of the Harvard Business School
On the other side of the river.
I could shoot the pope.
Last night I got drunk on champagne
& walked into a glass door
Looking for my lover
Though I'm not blaming her
That my nose is wide & hurts.
Full moon last night
In Taurus. I drank tons
Of champagne
Then I was sitting in
An all-night coffee shop
Eating my cheeseburger
When this black guy
Presiding
Over a group made
Some tiny statement
About the typical white female
So she said to him:
O, according to the
Average black male?

164

Two statistics addressing
One another
A little silence—nothing much.
O I really wonder
If I shouldn't go
To the hospital with this nose.
(I could hardly go without it
but that's hardly
the point. My nose hurts
and I feel sick
and nothing, nothing's new.)

>> <<

Last night by the champagne table
Rose is talking to this older french woman
Who says she's entirely celibate
& has decided for life & then
I get introduced to the woman
Who's decidedly cruising me.
Makes me think about the pope again
He maintained his stand on celibacy
—the big flirt. You know how
That works don't you? I mean
you know how easy it is for married
men to get laid. "I'm discreet."
I love you, you're so unique.
And *undemanding*. So later
I'm putting my arms around this
Celibate woman. I'm crazy
About integrity. That's
Why I'd like to shoot the pope.
And actually the guy
Who placed me on a napkin
Had only a few weeks earlier
Plowed a volkswagen
Into a telephone pole. I was
In that volkswagen. With
My friend Sally & this
Napkin guy & that volkswagen

Were all in cape cod.
So this guy starts taking
Me on dates & placing me on napkins
& finally he told me how
The accident *really* happened.
That's what history means to
A woman like me. There
Were so many woman in the room
Last night. I loved it—
I hardly danced. I danced
Slow once with my lover
And another high school dance
Collapsed inside my head.
That's the beauty of a lesbian.
Each one of us undoes history
A little bit & that's a lot.
Do you know we are the new
Nation? do you know we are
The Anti-Christ? That's what
It means. Both she & I
Decided that. Independently
Then we told each other &
In the happy shock it was true.
Do you know what it's like
When two women make love
Under a full moon? The
Light comes in waves.
Debussy had his fauns
In the afternoon
And it's really very lovely.
And I even wrote a
Poem to the sun once.
In the grand male tradition.
I used to think the thing to do
Was to be a women doing
All the things that poets do.
Talking to the sun & all that shit.
"Hello—this is a woman speaking."
When I told her I was planning
To shoot the pope—she said

"And in that moment,
You would know what it was like
To be a man. One such recognition
Would stop history I think.
The day seems to be lightening up.
I was going to ask him if
He needed more light—he's
Reading the Sunday Times in bed
But now the sky is brighter
& it's flowing into here.
Earlier we were in the bar
And she asked me how it
Was and I said, *well*
She asked me if I still love
her ... *and*   "Of course
I still love you"   I'll
Always love her and her face
Brightened. Whose? The one
I was talking to. In the bar
We were all popping Zoom
And then we went to the dance
In the room where all
The women were. Still are I bet.
That's why you should always
Leave early. I remember
—a full room. And a full
Moon—where is she, where
Is she—*Slam*. Right into glass.
Couple of years ago I was going
Up to the podium to read *Me*
And I walked smack into a mirror.
Imagine. I wrote *Me* when I was
Was yelling at her and now she's
My very best friend. We seem
To know one another's minds.
                    She was drunk
Too last night. But anyhow so
I went home & she was in
Bed & stroked my nose. And here
I am today. Just arrived.

167

Smoked my last cigarette again
So here I am at the crux again
Blam   the place where it always starts.

GENEVIEVE

One boring March evening
my parents were
trying to think
of something
to do since
Dad was sober
for a change
they decided to fuck.
At that moment
I got an idea
wrestled with it
finally
said, Ok, fuck, I'll try it.
That was in December.
Now we're in May
& still don't know
what to do. I wish television
existed in 1949.
It would've been Bilko
instead of me
and you'd be doing something
else right now.
You understand my problem
I suppose. Why this?!
and the leaves shake
it's getting light again
that's how it always starts
—you get caught up again.
Memories are for lovers
but I really don't know one
who isn't like my mother
really telling the same story
over & over again
until someone decides

to leave home. If Mom left town
the kids would have a house.
All the runaway notes
I left in childhood
were just substitutes
for Mom will you please leave.
But here I am getting
caught up in my own story.
I need a teevee
or to be in a series
—Lesbian Mother
a cute thirty-five year old woman
living with her collected kids
in a covered wagon
turning them on to booze
& shit. A very human drama.
To be very real you have to be
full of shit. Like the
streets. Why don't you run for Mayor
you slob, and clean this
town up! I'm very embarrassed for us.
I won't bring my kids
up in this mess.

1980: The Year of the Ox

I was just in this room
where one friend of mine
just quit smoking & this guy
was smoking Camels & another
woman was smoking ginseng
I laughed at her & asked for one.
Two women were walking around
the juicer—one wasn't bad-looking
the other one was sort of yellow
or orange, sallow, scary.
I thought she looked like death.
I thought—that ain't health.
This year I discovered that
it's fun to have a body—
something to be vain about.
I knew that when I was 19
but somehow or other
I forgot. Anxiety gets sexy.
To a point. Then I'll
start drinking & smoking or something
but at least until then
I'll let the barometer rise
the energy gets me around.
I'm into being a day animal
at night I can slow down
& look out of the corners
of my eyes. At the night.
It's a scurrying animal I think
feels like a bat sometimes
or any very dark bird alternately
sailing towards & against light.
I suppose I'm looking for a woman
—rowing in the old night boat.
I like the dark water, trying

to imagine where you'd go tonight
or else just throwing
my head back
watching the sky
wishing I could eat
all
those flowers.

from

A FRESH YOUNG VOICE FROM THE PLAINS (1981)

DAWN

I feel one tit
   well I feel two
     erratic taps in my room radiator
       taps in my speakers
    so early and deep blue
I should have gotten out
    before I was in

   now I see trees going bare
against blue autumn sky
     I see me   I see me again.

THIS EVENING

for Ted Berrigan

intense restlessness
and soon down the street   I should greet
you and declare I'm too young to die
should retire into extreme happi
ness

Look I'm sick
and should suck on a root. Ginseng
of course. Is there health after
death? I ask you that.
After 9 months of Ballet lessons
I resumed tomboyhood to piss
off my mother. It did
and I missed the lessons terribly.

Boom Boom Boom
My feet are loud tonight. Take the message
the moon is not out.
My light blue coat is
not the sky and sparkling
stars. Hello.

Hello.

TITLED

As I am poor
I intend to smoke my cigarette
Then the dinner is ready
But now I shall smoke

As I am rich I will rap
You in bluest silk
In another room
I imagine your beauty

O I despise the imagination!
A hard suck on the present
Basket of fears
And suggested blossoms

No I am not in the market for "posies"
It's late at night and
With my deep scope pressed

The skies are blooming
I can see it

Its beauty is the beauty of time

Encouraging

If I'm more stylish than I suspect
I like the gorgeousness of new.

MEDIUM POEM

I was the second of three children.
Born in middlesex county. Smack
in the middle of the twentieth century.
I have no womb memories
to the point of doubting my tenancy.
After-life seems a dubious conjecture.
I'll tell you when I get there. Paus-
ing in the middle of ladders
I smoke a cigarette for Wednesdays
when I am comfortable. And it is always
Wednesday. And I am never
sure. And I am always here.

OSSINING CORRECTIONAL FACILITY

I look in the ashtray and
see seven cigarettes. Each cigarette
is good for ten minutes.
I have listened to four tapes
thirty minutes each. Approximately
half the time I have sat in
this room I have been smoking.
The wind's rocking the windows
like wild. The young blond guard
who's sitting here with me is handsome.
He may be two years younger
than me. Anyhow we went to
gradeschool at the same time.
Approximately.
I imagine he's married.
Ossining is upstate is like Arlington
where I came from and
if I still lived in Arlington
I would be married.

Before I sat in this room I sat in another room. An old
balding lieutenant spoke with
me there. I had a subpoena
for him. To acquire some papers.
He said he had no papers.
The prisoner named Arthur had gone someplace
else.
Prisoners come and go all day
busloads of them
from Orange County, Westchester
some from the city but the lieutenant
does not have to accept them from the city.
He keeps twenty-four cells empty.
He will take fifteen from the city and

179

nine from the counties. Continually
these men come in and out
a lot on Friday, the counties
like to clean out their cells
over the weekend. Clean cells.
The lieutenant has one empty cell
block. Five or six full ones.
The old one should be knocked down
it's ancient he says. His eyes say
more. I know it's awful in that
block, used to be worse.
There used to be many more
men in this prison.
Now they shift in and out. The
lieutenant is paternal, soft and
rounded. His eyes say more.
There is a gleam that makes
my insides creep.
I flash on those busloads of
prisoners shifting in and out,
imagine the road I came to
Ossining Correctional Facility in a cab (Another
good business. Cabs wait at the train
station, wait at the prison seventy-five cents a head
even if the cab is full.)
and I imagine myself in a prison cattle-
bus shifting from prison to prison
it is very grey in Ossining. The
prison looks like a huge Dachau
on a hill overhanging a large grey lake.
It's very windy. My cab wound
up the hill to Ossining Correctional Facility
and flashing back I am prison cattle
cutting through greyness arriving here
and the lieutenant
has a quality that makes me
squirm and feel ill.

I am starving as I reach the train station
having taken another cab. This one is

180

free since I walked half the way
and cabs in this town are either
going to the prison or going to the train
station. Fine. So I can have a free
lunch on my bosses. It's three thirty and
I'm starving. I go to a small grocery
store where the counter lady is perhaps
deaf. Speaks in muffled muted squawks.
I ask for a quarter pound of swiss cheese and
a can of seven up. Ninety-five cents. I'm a nickel
ahead of the game.
I eat the swiss cheese greedily
like the large mouse that I
am.   I think about John
Cheever who I believe lives
in Ossining New York and of course
is haunted by the spectre of this
prison. In fact his latest suburban
novel is about just that. Another
writer I will never read never need.
John Cheever   John Cheever

I will never think about you again for
the rest of my life. And Ossining Correctional Facility
is not a spectre, it's a prison.

As I was being led out of the
prison by the blond guard
I passed by an alcove full of prisoners.

I froze for a second thinking I
would pass through that alcove.

I could feel their hungry hands on me.
I scrambled to the train station and
ate my cheese.

GREECE

This summer
I tell my friends
I intend to spend
a solid month
in Greece.

This is ridiculous
my friends say.
Look at yourself.
Your shoes are worn thin.
When rent time comes
you fall down in the street
and cry
until someone comes along
drops dollar bills on you.

I will go to Greece.
For a solid month.

Living on a Greek isle.
Bordered by the blue Aegean.
In a small stone house.
I can go to Greece
if I want.

On July 1st
sitting in my apartment
with my sandals on
I will be in Greece.

This is madness
my friends say.
You cannot travel by sheer

182

desire.
I agree with them. It's madness.
But in Greece I will be sane.

AUGUST 26

couple of honchos
   in a dark
     brown car on
      east 4th St.
getting high I
   suppose.

      I'm just
      admiring
      the indenta-

tions of the
   buildings on this
     street
funny how nobody
   probably imag-
     ines them-
selves living on
   a curve,

     middle, beginning
     or far end.
They just think
   of it all
   as their
   walls.

      I've always as-
      sumed
      myself

      to be an early or
      a late re-incarnation,
      my first life

or my
last.

Everything glows
like I've already
known it or
am I just a
dazzled baby
smug
and pretending
I've been
here before.

MY CHEAP LIFESTYLE

After a bourbon
I came in turned on the tube
Lit a joint and watched Monterey Pop
Nearly wept when Janis came on
Janis' legs kicking on stage is a memorable sight
Janis does her sweet little Texas girl smile as
Her act finishes. She kicks her heels
And Otis Redding is so sexy.
Millions of young americans experience religion for the first
    time
In their lives
Or so the cameras would inform us
I'm concerned about manipulation in this media
How one gains such wonderful power
But of course I'm too tired
Thrilled by the process of bringing down a familiar blanket
Upon my bed
It's nearly fall
Nearly winter
I expect the stars will be bright
The woods full of bears.

ON THE DEATH OF
ROBERT LOWELL

O, I don't give a shit.
He was an old white haired man
Insensate beyond belief and
Filled with much anxiety about his imagined
Pain. Not that I'd know
I hate fucking wasps.
The guy was a loon.
Signed up for Spring Semester at MacLeans
A really lush retreat among pines and
Hippy attendants. Ray Charles also
Once rested there.
So did James Taylor …
The famous, as we know, are nuts.
Take Robert Lowell.
The old white haired coot.
Fucking dead.

CONTINUITY

as composed as that graveyard over there.
Look how the rain spatters each stone and how the grass
curtly sprouts, how the tree unthinkingly drops
leaves like soggy baseball mitts. See how silent
the stones remain white-faced, grey-faced,
authoritatively obscure in their fierce one-liners.

The walls of the graveyard are stodgy and shy.
Rigid mommas sticking to their guns, how unthinkable
to guard cattle, separate neighbors, entwine children in
momentary recess, how much nicer the dead and their
     apparent
teeth, how ludicrous the fleshy ones who bring flowers
and self-interest. And the children who come
with their television eyes, beach-feet.

SWAN PLACE

I am running home fast as hell.

Or I am walking very slow.
            Whatever
        elucidates.   Mr.
Matheson has lost his nose. Lilian Matheson
is a nice snoop, Billy looks like a
chink and he lifts his cuffs swift-
ly and says "Nellie Fox ...
of the White Sox!!"

            Over on Pleasant Street
next to the old white church is
the burial place of Ebenezer Swan.

Mrs. Dingwell lives in the largest
house on the street. As does
Mrs. Wright the street's largest
woman. She has little boyfriends
a son named Jimmy with slicked back hair
a paper route and Jimmy took Billy
Le Blanc into the cemetery to see
the inside
            of a family vault.
        The Delays live next door to us.
Eight of them, many red-heads, very
skinny, Lady is their dog as was
Duchess who went to dog heaven
the first dog I knew who that
                        happened to.

        The Wyses
on the other side of the fence,
            Lombard Terrace,

conked Duchess on the head with a
baseball bat. Once when I
wanted to see what Russell and
David Wyse were doing I peeked
over the fence and got slapped
in the face by a dead eel. Russell
Or David threw it.   Or
maybe one of the Erkharts.

       Marbles   were introduced into
the neighborhood by the Delays,
       mainly Dickie. My brother
and I would go to the 5 & 10 and
          buy more
     and more
     cat's eyes. And whenever
Ruthy or Patty or Dennis Delay were
    losing at marbles Dickie
    would step in and win all
    the marbles.

    The Delays wore no sox
in the summer. Bare feet in sneakers
I pointed at their feet
when they first moved in and
      said   "You
don't have any sox on."
"Get out of our yard,
    you little snob!"
    Dickie said.

The older girls were Dottie,
   Helen and Gracie. Helen's
boyfriend was Koocha who had
a blue convertible and a heart
in black and red on his arm.

    Grace went steady with
Greg Testa, short and fat from
Somerville. Mrs. Delay, also Grace,

called Greg a ginnie.

Dottie always dated
sailors, she married one and they
moved to Fairbanks, Alaska.

Lawrence is the oldest. He drives
fast comes in late. Whenever
the fire-engines sirens are
going through the Center Lawrence
jumps in his car and chases
them. "Fire-bug" my mother says
as she sits on the porch with
my father playing scrabble.

The Delays know my mother
always sits on the porch or is
always looking down the street. They
call her "nosey Mrs. Myles." Just
the older daughters. Mrs. Delay
calls my mother "Mylesie" and
my mother calls her "Grace,"
my father says "Grace is a
good scout."

The Delays taught me to fish.
We go down to Spy Pond and
go to the rich people's docks
and catch carps. The people
don't mind, they say its
OK if we're quiet. We also
go deep sea fishing off the
boardwalk on Castle Island. They
catch crabs, I catch nothing but
love the boardwalk or going anywhere
with the Delays.

We walk all over Arlington.
We go to Menotomy Rocks Park or we
walk to Cambridge on the train

tracks we talk about running
away. We will steal horses from
the triple A stables in Medford
buy cowboy hats and go to
Texas. We draw maps on little
pieces of paper write goodbye
notes to our mothers. We
go home for supper when the
six o'clock train comes.

The Delays all go to public schools.
They are Catholic but they go to
public schools. They call me a
know it all and a show off because
I wear a blue uniform and go
to St. Agnes and can spell and
read better than them. I
would rather go to Parmenter with
them. I went to kindergarten
there. It is smaller, brighter
the books are prettier, you
can wear clothes, don't
have to memorize things, or
pass the Palmer Method,
they have an Art Room and
teachers not nuns.
Lorraine Fleming goes to Parmenter, too.
She lives on Swan Street, has a brother
Big Bill and a little sister Eileen
named after me.

        The Flemings house is
big. They have boarders, Katherine,
Mrs. Beatty, Louise, they are all
Mrs. Fleming's friends. They sit in
the kitchen and drink coffee with
her and she smokes cigarettes all
the time and she does the *Record
American* crossword puzzle.
Their house is very dark, Mr.

Fleming never talks. He sits
in front of the TV at five
o'clock and eats his supper
on a folding tray. Everyone in
the Flemings' house eats
different things. Billy is fat, Eileen
is fat, Lorraine is skinny and
always lying down. I go to
her house, call Hi-O Lorraine.
Mrs. Fleming likes me, tells me
Lorraine is upstairs. Lorraine is
in bed or on the toilet. So
I sit on her bed or on the
tub while she's going to the
bathroom and I try and get
her to go out. She always
goes out once she has
toast but she gets cranky
and doesn't like to run, shinny
up poles climb trees. The
Delays make fun of her.

Once when the Delays had
a crazy dog named Sparkle they
said "Sic her, Sparkle!"

Sparkle bit Lorraine in the fanny
and ripped her shorts. Lorraine
went home crying
and the Delays all laughed.
It was an accident, Sparkle
didn't even know what "Sic"
meant.

DESIRE IS JUST LIKE A PARKING LOT

Desire is just like a parking lot.
I know that for sure.
Last time I was there
I was a real meteorite.
Burned a hole in my soul.
That's why I now describe it as a parking lot.
I can see clearly now.
The whole wide universe is all the same.
All the people are the same.
No one's better than me.
Sure as hell she's not.
I'm no better than anyone.
Of course I condescend to some
Suck up to others.
I'm not out of touch with the powers that be.
Though when I think how each power is a tiny power
I get lost.
Standing in the middle of my parking lot.

WELSH POETRY

Mainly it's the shape of the hills as the old soldier laments
Three blue cars rush by
In this, New York City, all of us are heroes!

Whose green eye is upon my tennis shoe
Three birds land upon my firescape O love
My bewilderment is blind, has no season.

Three dogs are barking from three blocks away
Cool August wind blows through my sly silver screen
The year is latening, Hush, hear the dogs again.

VERSION OF COMPLAINT

For the past two weeks I've been bleeding
It's the longest running menstrual period
I've ever had

I'm horribly in debt
Was informed by the dentist my gums
Need lots of work

Still I get told I'm
The specimen of health

Am receiving tons of attention
In my particular intention

But I feel vividly alone
Can't seem to move
Towards the people I want

Like my desires a galloping horse
Only I hear it running

I do most things pretty well

Feel pride in my accomplishments
See it shine in your eyes!

This is just a hump I'll soon get over
I keep my defects around to
Stay on edge

But I'm bleeding!
I'm incredibly broke!

My gums My gums what will I do without my gums?
What will I hang my teeth on?

196

NEW YORK

I came here because I
wanted a home and
New York is the biggest home
you could possibly have.
Here I sit in a pizza joint
near Penn Central
my bag poignantly stuffed
& sitting on the stool to my left.
A pretty-old woman sits to my
right & I asked her
if she wanted something &
she said, No thanks I've al-
ready had mine. Hmmm
hope I can say that. To
her right is an immigranty-
looking youngish guy, a double-
knit shirt, the cuffs too long.
He'd be handsome in his
native land but here his
eyes are lost &
deeper in his head than they
should be. Also his coloring
which should be golden is
merely grey. Too bad. My
train should just be leaving.
Penn Central & back
is not romantic but
simply strange. I am the
prisoner of New York. It's
like in high school & college
when I was unable to quit
for fear of getting lost. Flapping
my wings madly in a void.
So I stayed pointlessly in

school or now, in this big home, my living room.
I love the giant library, 57th Street
on Sat. afternoon, St. Marks
Place late at night, Sheridan
Square in the early morning
… New York you are so
stagey, you suit me. I
am your pointless prop.

Bars: Grassroots, the Duchess, Fanelli's
I like the Colonnades, sometimes
the Locale, Spring Street sucks
but the food is good. I've only
been here 4 years so I shouldn't
talk like a lifer. Being a lifer
though is an attitude I think.
I would contrast my temporary
permanence with the light-heartedness
& ease of several actual
long-term residents of
correctional facilities. I once
worked in the correctional racket.
Also I worked as a librarian for
The American Stock Exchange, a
research assistant ("gopher")
to Stock Research Inc., cur-
rently "writer slash reporter" for
Orthovision. My task is to write
a piece of high-minded hype
for Orthovision saying something
to the effect that they
alone are doing reasonable humanitarian
transmissions into the colossally overloaded
spectrum of NYC.
Otherwise I've been a bouncer
then a waitress at the West End
Bar, Spring "Natural" (though
quite the reverse was true!)
and the Tin Palace. I worked
for the Vorpal Gallery one summer

putting up posters in windows
all over New York. M. C. Escher,
yecch! Someone who people
who like chess would probably enjoy.
I sold subway slugs for a year.
I retail blue diet pills
from a sleazy snake of a doctor
Stanley Beagle of Main Street
Flushing. I earned a
hundred and forty dollars this
year for reading poems. I
earned fifty dollars this year
writing poems. I spent 950 dollars
in 1978 on printing poems.

I've changed my milieu—now
in McCann's a corned beef &
beer bar, dark & cheap. These are
fine places as if the Boston bar
became an institution, that is a
chain. Sipping some soda
I'm cooling out. For 1 month
this summer I cooled out On
The Wagon   let my eyes clear
& see how genuinely apathetic
I feel towards Life. That's what
health is all about. Aiming
for health is true decadence
I think. I'm sure to have
serious bouts with it through-
out my life. But last night
I had 5 whiskeys & talked
pornographically with a friend
and then danced a lot with
her, and then took off & shot up
zowie, came home & she was
there but we just slept. Thank
you heroin.

So where was I going? Oh,

I was saying how I live in
New York. I was thinking how
I've been accused of having a
big mouth and I suppose it's
true. If I don't tell everyone
I'll put it in a poem. Or both
if it was good or bad enough.
But listen: if I talk about
you it's only I'm bragging how
lucky I am to have
gotten it on with you. That's
praise, you jerk. If you're
simply embarrassed to be
associated w/ me in that context
well then what can I say?
Tough shit.

New York is my home & that's what
I wanted so what am
I talking about?
I'm not free. Free to leave.
I feel like the Empire State Bldg.
I feel like a cartoon across
the surface of this city & strangely
have no interior life but
an external vision even
to myself. It gets horrible
sometimes. So I plan
to get more inward, keep
more secrets, leave this
town & come back, I don't
know. It's like a Pre-
Columbus vision in which
this city is flat (as I am)
and if you venture to
its edges you might fall off.
If you travel to foreign waters
you may encounter sea-dragons.
Or outside of it you are no one.
Ego extends to the perimeters

200

of NYC and not forsaking
EGO, unable to leave NYC
you sit still. Sit very
still. Then you pick up your
bag and *move*. An American
Optimist, yup.

Then, entering the subway, pushing through
the crowds at 34th, I saw a
baby sucking desperately on its bottle,
tears streaming down its fat dark face.
As it sat in its carriage. It stopped me,
I turned, examined some flowers
for sale, cloth on silky green leaves
mounted on a comb. I plucked
up a black one, a black rose, paid the
guy a dollar. I love it.

I'm softly fingering its petals on the
subway home, it is so artificial
so dark and so beautiful.

ALONG THE STRAND

for Steve Levine

When I was a coke-dealer
I just snorted all the profits.
Or like the time I fell in love
with Morning, it was something
I could stay with. I would
stick around but it slipped
into noon and again I fell in love

   at twilight I was meditative
and prayerful and by night I
was truly in love with someone
I could not see.

The person who invented inventions
was the same one who
waited to see what everyone was
requesting and then she invented

inventing. I tasted that once
but now it is no longer new.

The countermen placing chairs atop
tables, the tables are clean
and the radio plays all the new
songs.

What night was it that you told me
how the last time you felt this
way you just walked and walked

well I am the ghost of the coffee
shops who started smoking

very late. My father told
me they cause cancer and
I still believe they cause
cancer.

There is something wonderful about
plastic tables that resemble wood
and I am dreaming of a tree
by a stream that resembles
plastic.

For I am inventing again.

And I am walking backwards.
I grow deeply religious
as a child and as a
well-adjusted nun I am grateful
to the child who grew
me.

I am grateful to Dad's tip-
off concerning cigarettes, and
believing in denouements your footsteps
have stopped—you are
gladly resting on your couch.

Vouching for the honesty of
morning, he left me, became
someone else who I found be-
neath a plastic tree at
noon. Vigorous twilight is
our resting place and

we will exchange glowing photos
in the night.

Invention produces
pools and they are not in
demand.

I am endlessly walking and
a solid colored day is more
to my liking.

"You are my sunshine
my only sunshine"

        the singing voice
produces color, shades her
day. She is a nun of my
love who draws bands of
smoke which is prayer

I snorted all the profits. I
sleep on a pillow which is
my nose, I find it very
            religious.

my mother taught me sex was
dirty, which was exciting

she taught me love is romantic

I didn't start fucking till quite late.
Exciting, romantic,
I am quite sure it is the one
thing I have invented.

The times of the day, the ones
with names, they are the
stripes of sex unlike romance
who dreamlike is a continuous
walker,

obviously a solid colored day
is unexciting

I bring my best romance
to morning. I bring my best
romance to noon. Night

204

the old charmer is in love with
candles. Holds a fistful of
morning behind his back.

So you are no longer walking.
And this is no particular cigarette.
A beautiful nun may be dreaming
my life

　　　　or I am inventing again.

In ancient greece a mystical
child examines three ribbons.

The oldest woman in this part of
town is aware of her hair.

Black white and grey. Even
as she lay dying. Even as
she first fucked and her lover's
words caressed her like smoke, inventing
pools in her gorgeous and tangled
black hair.

A BRIEF STORY ABOUT MY FAMILY

my father's name was terrence myles
my grandfather's name was terrence myles
my older brother's name is also terrence myles.

my own name is eileen myles
named after an operetta
my parents were fond of
while they were dating.

my sister's name is ann myles
we call her nancy.
my mother and father felt they had to
call her ann.
there is no St. Nancy.

SKUPPY THE SAILOR DOG

I was just thinking about influential books in my life. Most of them were illustrated. I am thinking about one in particular, right now, unmootly titled "Skuppy the Sailor Dog." The plot was, or is, a little vague. Skuppy was a wandering sort of dog. Sailed the seven seas, made cameo appearances in various spots, one of which comes to mind is Turkey. Skuppy is standing is a sort of medina where he purchases a pair of purple slippers with curled up toes. How astonished I was at the thought of a dog inserting his paws in such shoes. Skuppy is never shown actually wearing the shoes.

They do appear in one scene in Skuppy's small mildly lit bunker. At this point in his life, it seems Skuppy is in ownership of his own small tug. He is lying on the lower bunk of a two-decker and is quite alone and somehow you feel he is alone on the entire boat, it is his boat.

Yet the lighting is all right. A single sailor's lantern hangs on the wall, a tawny cozy yellow sprays around the room in a warm twinkling. The purple shoes lie discreetly at the foot of his bunker, his striped sailor's shirt folded neatly on a single wooden chair.

He's asleep at this point, with an ever so slight smile coursing his mouth, more of a glow than a smile.

Having good dreams, other places, countries, infinite new shoes to buy and strange people to purchase from. It is night of course and the boat is softly at sea, moving on its own correct course. Storm-free and guided by Skuppy, smiling at his dreaming.

TEXAS

I'm nearly crying for it—
looking at the large coloured map on his wall
poor TEXAS looking big-as-life
and dying to secede
Mama, did Annie Oakley ever cry?   Or,

Mother is it true she couldn't cry
that's why she could shoot so well?

O Mama,
I just want to cry
sitting here looking at TEXAS across
the face of the map

so big & so lonely
I just want to get a beebee gun
and shoot that fucking state to bits

SWEET CHINA

I threw the *I Ching* and
I thought about you and I threw
the *I Ching* and
I thought about you

First it said "Armies,"
then "The Marriageable Maiden"
and then it said
"The Abyss,"
then I thought about you

All along the *I Ching* kept saying
"Don't advance," "Don't Advance."
This afternoon
my friend on the phone
was telling me to do it.
There's no right time,
she said. I mean, you can
always try again.
I mean, I've got these
regrettes

they sound like little
blue-nosed flowers
wilting in my hands.
I mean, the coins are on the floor,
my hands are in my pockets, and I
keep smoking and smoking

THE HONEY BEAR

Billie Holiday was on the radio
I was standing in the kitchen
smoking my cigarette of this
pack I plan to finish tonight
last night of smoking youth.
I made a cup of this funny
kind of tea I've had hanging
around. A little too sweet
an odd mix. My only impulse
was to make it sweeter.
Ivy Anderson was singing
pretty late tonight
in my very bright kitchen.
I'm standing by the tub
feeling a little older
nearly thirty in my very
bright kitchen tonight.
I'm not a bad looking woman
I suppose   O it's very quiet
in my kitchen tonight   I'm squeezing
this plastic honey bear   a noodle
of honey dripping into the odd sweet
tea. It's pretty late
Honey bear's cover was loose
and somehow honey   dripping down
the bear's face   catching
in the crevices beneath
the bear's eyes   O very sad and sweet
I'm standing in my kitchen   O honey
I'm staring at the honey bear's face.

from

THE IRONY
OF THE LEASH (1978)

HOMEBODY

Oh, Hello. C'mon in.
You know, I was just thinking about how you've
Always thought I was *cool*…
And here I am, cooking fishcakes and broccoli.
I didn't know how I could re-present all this for you.
This is where I'm really at. Nothing's
As fetching as the raw.
I heard the dog barking on the third landing
& I was fairly sure it'd be you.
Kind of rainy out tonight. I was so exhausted
After work. Made some coffee
& sat here reading the Voice. Sort of
Thought I'd hear from you. I thought,
Well, he'll either be in the same mood
Or different. And look:
I've got a magenta sock and a rust
Sock on. Just like the, uh, Futurists.
And my old workshirt. Feels good
Since it's clean for a change.
Oh, do you want some? The broccoli's
Good with grated cheese on it. Yeah,
The fishcakes suck,
But just douse them with lemon juice.

January 28

MISOGYNY

"My new tack will be to hate women,"
I uttered to Ann,
my voice quivering with discovery.
"But, Eileen ... you *are* a woman,"
my sister Ann uttered back,
the usual disdain creaking through the air.
"That's the only hitch ..." I slowly sighed

and another near adventure was bypassed.
Like *Melanctha*, this evening's paper adventure,
I crave excitement, even if it's throwing twigs
into my own conflagration, damn it,
I missed Dreyer's *Joan of Arc* tonight.
At 8:15 I was speaking with Richard
watching the minute hand sweeping away
that silent evening. I am prepared

to be a saint but I received a pamphlet in the mail
last week, concerning sainthood, concerning
the particular sainthood of Mother Seton
and I learned that sainthood does not mean
"... that the Church recognizes that a Catholic
convert has 'made good' by American standards;
it means that an American
wife, mother, educator,
religious convert to Catholicism and heroic woman

has 'made good' by God's much more exacting standards.
It is ample reason for American rejoicing ..."
I dash into the kitchen in search of beer.
Oh no. The green quart of Ballantine was killed
last night. I slip on my green sweater and things seem
to grow balanced. Richard borrowed this sweater once
stretched the shit out of it

but the point is he never wears green and everybody
noticed. There are colors like that there are things
I could just never say. Perhaps you are bothered
by my thumb scraping across this balloon or
the cutting of cardboard disturbs. Sounds of squeaking
styrofoam would convince me to betray my deepest
secrets and sometimes writing poems
I hope I would undo those sounds.

Mayonnaise is offensive and I hate gold jewelry
sitting on tables while I eat. I remember how you grimaced
at the smells in my hallways
and I added a check on your manifold paranoia. It's nice
           to dance with women but nobody's aiming. And
                red hats
only cause internal discomforts and short coffee breaks
tomorrow. What would John Ashbery say at a time like this?
     A tick-
ing that improves with the gleaning. Some eagerness, of
     course,
is gathered up with tomorrow's wash and a meal with several
     friends.
The globe sits with some luminosity on whose bureau. OK,
so next time I'll try Rudyard Kipling. Barbara Walters.
John Keats. Ronald McDonald. Bernadette Mayer. Melanie
     Haber.
Moonbeam McSwine. Brenda Starr. Raymond Burr. Eric
     Roehmer.
Bill Zavatsky. Andrew Carnegie. Sybil Burton.
Sally Fields. Flannery O'Connor. Flann O'Brien. Myles
     naGopaleen.
Topaz Magillacuddy. Little Lulu. Barbara Guest.
Rosalind Russell. Barbara Walters.
Barbara Walter. Walter de la Barbara. Walter de la Mare.
Art Carney. Jackie Gleason. Art Carney. Jackie Gleason.
Art Carney. Jackie Gleason.
Trixie. Lily Tomlin. Trixie. Lily Tomlin.
Trixie. Lily Tomlin.
Trixie. Trixie. Trixie.
Pixie. Trixie. Pixie. Trixie. Spot. Puff. Rover.

Duke. Duchess. Foo-Foo. Prince.
Queenie. Bourbon. Romulus. Remus.
Blackie. Constance.
Fido. Pixie. Fido. Pixie. Trooper. Humble.
Amelia. James. Anonymous.

BLACK LACINGS

Bon Ami, the shiftless one, walked grimly across
the beach, his white sneakers
glowing like the moon. Black branches lacing his view.
He had lost his baby-blue kite
& the sky was grey today. His sneakers shone
like a white moon. His thoughts
were a black tangled fish-net
darting at wild angles like the charcoal sketches
of the retarded. How white were his sneakers.
They glow like the moon. Not just any moon.
A Charles Simic moon. A tall glass of milk.
    Clutter of driftwood alerted him.
It was brown like his old bathing suit.
It was wooden like brown wooden trees.
"Mixing of elements," he murmured.
Sand and wood. Sand and blue sky.
Blue sky and my glowing sneakers.
Combinations came faster and shiftless Bon Ami
felt like god. He felt confused.
Ambling home grinning at his sneakers.
He aimed to soak them in moon-glow again.
Tonight. If the front porch was free.

Onwards Upwards & Always

Nobody could deny no other bad times.
An electric torch as a matter of course, a mixed blessing.
Marvelously up to date, June 10th.
33 dogs under the sea. They had slept in their clothes.
"This entailed."
In a fortnight they were obliged to spend a second summer
In the hut under the active volcano. 25 of them
Living there, really ill, complaining of stuffiness
And too many lectures, 3 a week.
Trustful by nature, sun-up was by 7. Cherry Garrard,
Sometimes a latin dictionary, is not a complete answer.
They said no. Their loyalty to each other was fantastic.
Full of light and shade, no beer.
Very funny indeed.
Hooker died that *very* year, 1911. An adorable person,
The egg of an emperor. Paternity
Is the only joy. Indiscriminately breaking and killing in the
    process.
On the coast everybody volunteered for everything.
They steered by Jupiter, the simplest action. I hope I have
    not
Disappointed him, a party of four.
Meant for four. He had eaten most of the dogs,
A hot stew, the bold way in which he met his death.
Now the weather changed, ordinary good luck.
My dear Mrs. Wilson: he died as he lived. The sun
Reappeared terribly soon
Smiling into cupboards.

EVENING

Supposed to be there at 7 o'clock.
It's 8 o'clock now. Better buy some beer.
Go in the door, Sorry I'm late Frank
Here's six apologies ...

Sit down at the table start drinking my words.
Start playing Parcheesi with his kid.
Who keeps revising the rules, the little cheat.
Keeps using my lighter. It's cheap
But so what ... he's irritating me.
We have some dinner, some steak, some rice,
(Call broccoli *trees.*)

Call the situation perfunctory and sweet.
We go look at poems, postcards, we
Drink coffee but the beer is still with us,

Wish I had some grass, wish I was someplace
                                                    else

Boring to be me, glad I'm not married,
I'd be a child-beater, glad I can go home.
I feel woozy,

                    Walk down

Gorgeous soft tree-lined streets in the
Dark. Cushy. As dark rows of trees
Are stroking the wind or
The wind's stroking them.

An Attitude About Poetry

My attitude about poetry is somewhat
this, I should be doing something
that pays more money.
I love comfort, bright things for myself
and the ability to splurge on people I
like, to be able to dislike
people who have bucks.

That is the poetry of money.
Money is a friend,
a comfy chair when you need to sit,
free walking. Buying rides.
Zoom in on this one.
Avoid that one in a helicopter ride
around Australia. Bury
my sorrows in an incredible meal.
You like that star. I buy you that car.
Never drunk but gliding on the
        ethers of everyone's
            drunkenness.
        It trips me up,
my lightweight love of cash,
    it clicks on my teeth.
        My words jingle.

CIGARETTES

Emotions are like clothes. As I'm putting mine on
and you're taking yours off. Today I wore total blue. And
what I was selling was blue. I kept them in a blue bag
and I didn't sell a thing. People passing by admiring all
the blue. Every morning

I throw cigarettes under the faucet. Every night
I'm licking salt from my fingers, ketchup from my clothes.
I can see good reasons for why MacDonald's exists. Constant
stage for out provocations to dance from. Andy Warhol
said it would be nice if all the cars were black. Creative
fascist pure beauty of streams of black traffic. And all
the brightly colored people coming in and out of cars.
Cigarettes are my pet degradation.
I smoke them so much that everything's smoke. Then I stop
and breathe up the excess. Do you need a match?
The tic and the tac go shrugging
and then you get toe. Fourteen cigarettes under the faucet.

CORIOLANUS

and I hadn't read any of the plays at all.
Last semester senior year. I therefore crammed
by starving myself and getting from Robbins Library
    recordings
of *Coriolanus* and *The Winter's Tale* and various others and I
    can't
remember if the course was the comedies and histories or
    the tragedies
perhaps you know
but I lay on the couch in the parlor for two days
hungry and listening to Shakespeare
I saved *Coriolanus* for the morning before the exam
I was drinking coffee and looking at the clock
allowing forty-five minutes to reach Harvard Square
about one quarter of the record was left
then Park Street either walking through the Common or
catching a trolley to Boylston
Richard Burton was in *Coriolanus* he was very good
the exam was not too bad I somehow divined a single grand
    theme
running through all of the plays and all of the plays
were one warbling mass to me with the artificial thunder and
false rain. I filled three blue-books and
got a C+ on the exam. I'm no prodigy.

GREEN

this is why it rains today
green always requires a form
nudging selves from inner chambers
hospital rooms would pretend some calm

green always requires a form
that is why it hails today
hospital rooms would pretend some calm
take some rest in the shadow of leaves

that is why it hails today
tapping of ice like disregard
take some rest in the shadow of leaves
calm is blades of growing dreams

tapping of ice like disregard
soft songs whisper beneath my window
calm is blades of growing dreams
that is why I sing today

soft songs whisper beneath my window
I grow my jokes in dazzling green
that is why I sing today
that is why my walls are green

I grow my jokes in dazzling green
green is abundant; needs no rest
that is why my walls are green
my walls are calm like growing dreams

green is abundant; needs no rest
this is why it rains today
my walls are calm like growing dreams
nudging selves from inner chambers

223

SUBSCRIPTION

Animals forever escaping
from zoos
& they will come to my door.
Too many masturbation manuals
are being written. Too much pie
passes over the counter. I bathe
in yellow light & dream of you.
I miss myself as the train
pulls out of a station in Jerez, España.

The Irony of the Leash

Life is a plot to make me move.
I fill its forms, an unwitting
                    crayon

            I am prey to the materials
of me, combinations
            create me into something
        else, civilization's inventions

numb me, placate me
            carry me around. I
am no better than a dog.
    My terms are not bark
            and howl

but I often get drunk and rau-
cous, often I need to get
laid so bad I imagine my
howls lighting up the neighborhood
            pasting rings
        around the moon.

As a child I was very in love
with the stars. As a human
        a victim of my perceptions
it is natural that I should love
light and as a passive dreamer

it is natural I should be attracted
to the most distant inaccessible
light. When do you make of
this. Friend? I need the reass-
                    urance

of human voices so I live with
a phone or I go out and seek
my friends. Now they are always
different, these people who
happen to be moved by the same
            music as me, whose
faces I like, good voices,

I can recognize the oncoming footsteps
of a person I like. In this
I am little better than a dog.

Sometimes I go to movies and I
sit in the dark. Leaving the light
and relishing the movements
            of images occurring
            in another time, bright
and pretty, sometimes gruesome

and violent and though I know
very well,
        (as I paid my 1.50 and came
in here and chose a seat
        a decision based on the condition
of my eyesight and my place
            in society
I may sit in the front or
the back, am I old,
            am I young ...)

I know very well that this movie is not
            real, yet I am often
in the grips of fears more real
than those my own life throws up
for my unwilling complicity

and I am visibly shaken, often
            nearly screaming with fright
and revulsion ...

yet I know it is not real.

Movies have caused me to become
an artist. I guess I simply
        believe that life is not
        enough. I spin dreams
of the quotidian out of words I
could not help but choose.

They reflect my educational background,
    the economic situation of
            my parents and the countries
their parents came from. My words
        are also chemical reflections:

metabolically I am either fast or
        slow, like short words or
        long ones, sometimes I
like words which clack hard against
    each other like a line of
            wooden trains. Sometimes
I wish my words would meld
to a single glowing plastic tube slightly
    defying time.   I write
quite a bit,

        I no longer believe in religion
but find writing an admirable
        substitute,
I don't particularly believe in art
but I know that unless there is
    something I do which is
at least as artificial and snide
            and self-perpetuating ...

well then I would have to find ·
someone else who
        had that sort of handle
on things and hold onto him
    for dear life.

I would be less than a dog.
I think it's important to have
        your own grip on
    things, however
that works and then you should
pursue that and spend the
        rest of the time
doing the ordinary.

Exactly like a dog. Dogs
are friendly creatures unless
    they've been mistreated.
They like to eat and run around.
They neither drink nor smoke
nor take drugs. They are perfect.
        They mate freely
whenever they have the urge.
They piss and shit according to
their needs, often they appear
to be smiling but of course
they are always happy.
Interestingly enough,
it is quite popular, particularly
in the city in which I live,
to own a dog, to walk him on a
                        leash
morning noon and night, people with
families have dogs and they add
        to the general abundant chaos
    of the household,

people who live alone own dogs. For
protection, regularity and
the general sense of owning a friend.
People love their dogs and undoubtedly
their dogs love them. Though
they are faithless and impersonal.
They love their owners because
they feed them, stroke them,
bring them outside to run around,

if a dog gets injured
its owner will take it to a doctor or
a clinic, depending on the economic
situation of the owner.

Dogs do not believe in God or Art.
Intrinsically they have a grip
on things.

I unfortunately do not. I sit
here with a bottle of beer, a cigarette
and my latest poem, *The Irony of the Leash*.

August 6

Printed June 1995 in Santa Barbara
& Ann Arbor for the Black Sparrow Press by
Mackintosh Typography & Edwards Brothers Inc.
Text set in Janson by Words Worth.
Design by Barbara Martin.
This edition is published in paper wrappers;
there are 200 hardcover trade copies;
100 hardcover copies have been numbered & signed
by the author; & 26 copies handbound in boards
by Earle Gray are lettered & signed by the author.

Photo: Jennifer Montgomery

EILEEN MYLES was born in Cambridge, Mass. in 1949, was educated in Catholic schools and graduated from U. Mass. (Boston) in 1971. She moved to New York in 1974 to be a poet. She gave her first reading at CBGB's and then gravitated to St. Mark's Church where she studied with Paul Violi, Alice Notley and Ted Berrigan. She edited a poetry magazine, *dodgems*, in 1977–1979. She ran the Poetry Project for a couple of years, 1984–1986. She's written two plays, *Feeling Blue, Pts. 1, 2 & 3* and *Modern Art*, both of which were performed at P.S. 122. Currently she's writing *Our Sor Juana*, a solo piece, based on the life of the 17th century poet nun of Mexico for the performance artist, Carmelita Tropicana. Black Sparrow Press published her book of short stories, *Chelsea Girls*, in 1994. Also Eileen Myles co-edited (with Liz Kotz) an anthology, *The New Fuck You/adventures in lesbian reading* for Semiotext(e) which will be out in 1995.